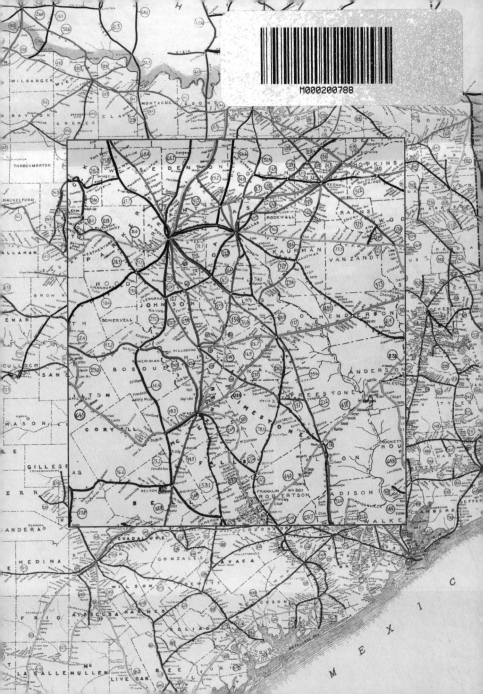

M000200788

FARMER CASTRO SWISHER BRISCOE HALL
BAILEY LAMB HALE FLOYD MOTLEY
COCHRAN HOCKLEY LUBBOCK CROSBY DICKENS KING
YOAKUM TERRY LYNN GARZA KENT STONE
GAINES DAWSON BORDEN SCURRY FISHER
ANDREWS MARTIN HOWARD MITCHELL NOLAN
LOVING WINKLER ECTOR MIDLAND GLASSCOCK COKE
CULBERSON WARD CRANE UPTON REAGAN IRION TOM GREEN
PETH REEVES STERLING
JEFF DAVIS PECOS CROCKETT SUTTON SCHLEICHER
PRESIDIO TERRELL
BREWSTER VAL VERDE EDWARD
KINNEY
MAVERICK

YELLOW
East Texas & Gulf Ry.
Groveton, Lufkin & Northern Ry.
Missouri Pacific Lines:
  Asherton & Gulf Ry.
  Beaumont, Sour Lake & Western Ry.
  Houston & Brazos Valley Ry.
  International-Great Northern R.R.
  Orange & Northwestern R.R.
  Rio Grande City Ry.
  San Antonio, Uvalde & Gulf R.R.
  St. Louis, Brownsville & Mexico Ry.
  Sugar Land Ry.
Moscow, Camden & San Augustine Ry.
Texas & Pacific R.R.
  Denison & Pacific Suburban Ry.
Texas Southeastern R.R.
Weatherford, Mineral Wells & North-
  western Ry.

ORANGE
Angelina & Neches River R.R.
Denison, Bonham & New Orleans R.R.
Fort Worth & Denver City Ry.
Texas City Terminal Ry.
Texas Midland R.R.
Trinity & Brazos Valley Ry.
Wichita Falls, Ranger & Fort Worth R.R.
Wichita Valley Ry.

BROWN
Chicago, Rock Island & Gulf Ry.
Eastland, Wichita Falls & Gulf R.R.
Nacogdoches & Southeastern R.R.
Paris & Mt. Pleasant R.R.

TEXAS

Cocktails

AN ELEGANT COLLECTION OF OVER

100 RECIPES INSPIRED BY THE

LONE STAR STATE

NICO MARTINI

CIDER MILL
PRESS

BOOK
PUBLISHERS

KENNEBUNKPORT, MAINE

Texas Cocktails

Copyright © 2018 by Appleseed Press Book Publishers LLC.

This is an officially licensed book by Cider Mill Press Book Publishers LLC.

All rights reserved under the Pan-American and International Copyright Conventions.

No part of this book may be reproduced in whole or in part, scanned, photocopied, recorded, distributed in any printed or electronic form, or reproduced in any manner whatsoever, or by any information storage and retrieval system now known or hereafter invented, without express written permission of the publisher, except in the case of brief quotations embodied in critical articles and reviews.

The scanning, uploading, and distribution of this book via the Internet or via any other means without permission of the publisher is illegal and punishable by law. Please support authors' rights, and do not participate in or encourage piracy of copyrighted materials.

13-Digit ISBN: 978-1604337686
10-Digit ISBN: 1604337680

This book may be ordered by mail from the publisher. Please include $5.99 for postage and handling. Please support your local bookseller first!
Books published by Cider Mill Press Book Publishers are available at special discounts for bulk purchases in the United States by corporations, institutions, and other organizations. For more information, please contact the publisher.

Cider Mill Press Book Publishers
"Where good books are ready for press"
PO Box 454
12 Spring Street
Kennebunkport, Maine 04046
Visit us online!
cidermillpress.com

Cover design by Cindy Butler
Interior design by Jaime Christopher
Typography: Avenir, Brothers, Copperplate, Sackers, Warnock
Image Credits: see page 365–366

Printed in China
1 2 3 4 5 6 7 8 9 0
First Edition

CONTENTS

INTRODUCTION

★ ★ ★ ★ ★ ★ ★ ★ ★

INTRODUCTION

"IF A MAN'S FROM TEXAS, HE'LL TELL YOU.
IF HE'S NOT, WHY EMBARRASS HIM BY ASKING?"

– John Gunther

Texans are always in good spirits. This is home and we're happy to be here. Those who surround us are family and our family comes first. We're a prideful, yet humble, lot of straight shooters that are the friendliest people you'll ever meet. If you're in a bar in Texas, I promise you that you'll come out with more friends than you walked in with, and you can hang your hat on it.

The first thing I did when I sat down to write this book was start researching all of the classic cocktails that came from Texas. I found both of them. I even cornered David Wondrich, the world's most celebrated cocktail historian, at a conference and asked him if I was missing anything. He told me about a commander at the battle of Sabine Pass who was also a saloon owner. (His name was Dick Dowling and his bar was Bank of Bacchus, one of the most popular places in Houston in the 1860s.) There was a journal that mentioned the names of some of the drinks, but no recipes. He said, "I did a bunch of research on Texas a while back and that's all I ever found."

Frankly, the only two cocktails I could find that legitimately come from Texas are the Chilton and the Ranch Water... and we built the frozen margarita machine, for which we are both sorry and not sorry. I decided that I would let the best bars and bartenders represent our state, and I'd do my best to get out of the way. Over a hundred cocktail recipes later, you have *Texas Cocktails*. This is a snapshot of Texas in 2017... but at the rate we're moving, it couldn't be done any other way.

Texas is the epitome of vast. I'm not going to say that everything is bigger here, but when you set out to represent the entire state, it sure feels that way. There are cocktail bars in LA that are closer to El Paso than McAllen is, and there are bars in Chicago that are closer to Texarkana than El Paso is. It's big here, y'all.

We're a little southern, a little western, a little Mexican, a little country, a little urban—a state with dramatic differences between our people, but where folks will fight tooth and nail for each other. We're American by birth and Texan by the grace of God. We've always been tough to categorize because we are our own category.

As for the cocktail scene, Texas has carved its own way. "There was nothing accidental about this," David Alan, author of *Tipsy Texan* and global brand ambassador for Patrón told me. "It was not just right place, right time. It was active and it was a lot of work. It was things like if the newspaper wrote something inaccurate about bartenders, we'd write a letter to the newspaper. If a magazine wouldn't correctly cover what you do, we'd start writing for the magazine. If the distributors did carry something, we'd start calling. None of this was an accident." We worked for this. It was sheer Texan want that made this scene possible.

We're proud here. Texans are some of the most loyal and most prideful people you'll ever meet. We're also ridiculously friendly. For Texans, we don't need to "get back to hospitality" as everyone else in

the country seems to be screaming because we were born hospitable. The laid back, easy going, friendly, warm nature of Texans is exactly why we're good at this. We have some of the most inventive bartenders in the country, who are rooted in friendliness. (Shoutout to Bombay Sapphire's Most Imaginative Bartender, Justin Lavenue from Austin.)

The Texas cocktail scene is world-class in approachability. The bars that are thriving right now are neighborhood bars that happen to have stellar cocktail programs. We've moved beyond the 9-touch craziness, dialed everything back, and made it incredibly easy to get a proper cocktail here. Our cocktails are for anyone and everyone. Not only is it now impossible to open a restaurant without a cocktail menu of some sort, but the drinks on that menu have been specifically built

to remove all intimidation. Even our most renowned bars were created to serve communities and not fads.

My great-grandfather came to Texas on a pony from Morelos, Mexico. In fact, the area where he stopped and set up shop had been Mexico less than 80 years prior. I've spent my entire life seeing the influence of Mexican culture on Texas, and it's been incredible to see its impact on the cocktail scene, specifically. You'll never convince me that Mexico—you know, the place where the tequila, limes, and agave come from—didn't invent the margarita. However, the margarita is, without question, the single most important drink in the state of Texas. The influence grows from there.

The staggering rise in popularity of tequila and mezcal? We might have had something to do with that. The idea of adding spice to cocktails? Hell, y'all's peppers aren't even hot. While the history of Texas spirits may start with Tito, we've been working with Mexican spirits since we were, well, Mexico.

We have the best grapefruit in the world. We have peaches that are rivaled only by Georgia. And look out Kentucky... but we're figuring this whiskey thing out pretty quickly. Just give us twelve more years to age it. I tried to honor the diversity of the state in the choices that were made for this book. I've tried to speak from my heart as a Texan and I've done my best to represent the state as a whole. The last thing I wanted to do was look at a map of where these cocktails came from and only see Dallas, Houston, Austin, and San Antonio. It's pretty incredible that it was even possible. You can get a great margarita in Webster. Midland makes proper Manhattans now. Denton and College Station, seminal Texas college towns, have classy joints where you can grab an old fashioned.

I asked David Alan what was different between when his book came out and now and he said "Didn't you just tell me that you found 101 different bars that serve proper cocktails? That's the difference." As

Jeret Pena told me, we won. Cocktails have won. Now it becomes a battle to stand out in this scene... and not one Texan I know is afraid of a little competition.

Honorary Texan Jason Kosmas told me, "I think Texas is training more cocktail drinkers, by far, than any coast." Makes sense, doesn't it? So until you can visit these bars yourself, which is an experience that cannot be matched, I hand you these recipes. I hand you over a hundred recipes I, unapologetically, did not write. I let the geniuses in this state do what they're good at and I got the hell out of the way.

HARVEYS FOR HARVEY

Hurricane Harvey was one of the most terrifying, costly, disastrous events to ever hit Texas. Entire communities under water, displaced people without homes, the smell of cut wood and mildew permeating the air... Can you genuinely imagine what it's like to be evacuated from your home as it is sinking into flood water, knowing that it's gone? Everything—every picture, every book, every favorite shirt, every teddy bear... gone. And at the time you're more interested in staying alive. And at the time you're trying to help your elderly neighbor. And at the time your adrenaline is so high that it never quite registers that you don't know if your insurance policy covers rising water.

At the time, you're too focused on saving others to realize that you've lost everything.

But you fight through, and the community around you rises up. The damage Harvey's inflicted cannot be undone, but the Gulf Coast community in Texas has united to help their brothers and sisters get through this. The same can be said for the service industry.

The Harvey Wallbanger is one of the most incredible initiatives I've ever seen. Over $250,000 was raised by bars and bartenders across the world to benefit the victims of Hurricane Harvey. Over 500 bars participated by doing what they do best... selling cocktails.

The Harvey Wallbanger is a simple drink that will now live in infamy. This is, in fact, a recipe book, so I thought I'd include it.

When Harveys for Harvey became a rallying cry, Lucas Bols, makers of Galliano, stepped up in a huge way. They donated all profits from the sales of Galliano in September to relief efforts in the greater Houston area. On top of that, they helped with publicity and coordination and they never asked for anything in return. I'm not writing this because I got a press release about it, I'm writing this because they made a difference.

Other brands matched donations or contributed products to fundraisers all over the state and the nation. The United States Bartenders' Guild San Antonio Chapter raised $15,000, and the Dallas Chapter raised over $40,000. There are thousands of members of "Service Industry for Harvey Relief" groups on Facebook and events are still happening.

The resiliency of the Houston service industry is a true inspiration, and the impact of these industry fundraisers is quite real. Bobby Heugel said it best, "Thank you to everyone that donated to help our city, bought a Harvey Wallbanger, or just did something for people anywhere in need this last month and a half. When you watch an event like this happen first-hand, you realize how small and helpless you are as an individual. And then, when you watch everyone band together and respond, humanity's real strength becomes apparent. There are currently and will be more challenges ahead—there always are. Our only real option for overcoming them is together."

The Harvey Wallbanger was, more than likely, the creation of a marketing team in the late 1960s. By 1969, the character "Harvey Wallbanger" appeared in everything from pop art to bumper stickers. This silly little cocktail began to appear on reputable cocktail menus again in the early 2000s after Galliano switched back to their original recipe.

Glassware: **Tall Glass**

- **1.25 oz vodka**
- **3 oz orange juice**
- **.5 oz Galliano L'Autentico**

1. Combine orange juice and vodka in a tall glass with ice.

2. Stir and float Galliano on top.

3. Garnish with an orange slice.

DRINK LIKE A TEXAN

How do you drink like a Texan? Grab a fajita and let's do this…

★ Your pregame is Topo Chico or Dr. Pepper. Or probably Shiner.

★ When you toast, you tap the table before you drink. Cheers to the future but acknowledge the past.

★ If it's a celebration, you're raising a glass. If it's a tailgate or it's a baptism, odds are there's a keg… and a surly uncle with a handle of whiskey.

★ Beer is the King, but Margarita is our Queen.

★ Cowboy boots are for every occasion. Whether you're at a black-tie gala or literally roping a calf, boots are the footwear of choice.

★ We like hot sauce on our hot sauce.

★ Our first drink was either a frozen margarita given to us as a tiny sip by our favorite aunt at a hole-in-the-wall Mexican joint, or a sip of beer at a family reunion, probably given to us by the same surly uncle who brought the handle of whiskey.

★ Our hospitality is as Southern as it gets.

★ If you're floating the river, your best raft holds the beer.

★ If you want to sneak booze into a football game, you put a flask in your boot. Everybody knows that.

★ Check your degree at the door. We don't care if you're a doctor or a ranch hand, no one pulls rank inside the bar.

TEXAS COCKTAILS SOUNDTRACK

Music is done a little differently in Texas. From the roots of outlaw country to some of the best hip hop in the nation, Texas music is as diverse as it's cocktails. I asked my friend Mark Schectman to help design the perfect soundtrack to cruise around to these great cocktail spots. He hosts a weekly new music radio show called 'The Local Ticket' that can be heard every Sunday night on Sportsradio 1310/96.7FM The Ticket in Dallas. He's the creator of #fancydranks and the proud owner of a super-secret speakeasy called The Hitchcock, which can only be accessed through his side yard. Mark once told me, "I like cocktails because they make me feel fancy." You and me both, pal.

Old 97's—Niteclub
An ode to the special relationship you have with your favorite bar...and the people that frequent that bar.

Ben Kweller - Wasted and Ready
We're not saying you shouldn't imbibe responsibly. We're also not saying that we've never felt this feeling before.

The Texas Gentlemen - Habbie Doobie
A raucous 6:17 exploration of Americana, honky tonk and good times.

St. Vincent - What, Me Worry?
There's nothing like a sweet song wrapped in an Arrested Development reference that sounds like a French 75 tastes.

Beyonce - 7/11
Pairs well with the "Hot Mess" from Vox Table in Austin (page 150) and the "What Really Happened" from Houston Watch Company (page 98).

Blue the Misfit - Child of the Night
Day drinking is fun and all, but some of us just hit another gear after the sun goes down.

Ghostland Observatory - Life of the Party
Shout out to the heroes that help the host clean up.

Son of Stan - Loseyomind
The king of divorce pop makes you wanna dance. Pairs well with awkward bar conversations and whiskey. Also it pairs well with the "Son of Stan" at Off the Record in Deep Ellum (page 346).

Charlie Crockett - Just a Drink Away
Dallas bluesman channels the memory of Ernest Tubb's tune about good ol' fashioned heartache.

White Denim - Corsicana Lemonade
Austin psychedelic prog-rock dabbling taking you on a tour of Texas with a lemonade in hand.

T-Bird and The Breaks - Blackberry Brandy
A little extra money, or a delicious drink? If only all choices in life could be this easy.

The Reverend Horton Heat - Please Don't Take the Baby to the Liquor Store
Don't tell me what to do, Rev. We've done this. You should too.

Lyle Lovett - That's Right (You're Not From Texas)
A tune about Southern (Texan) hospitality. Even if you're not from Texas, we're glad you're here.

Pat Green - Take Me Out to a Dance Hall
Ahh alcohol...As the philosopher Homer J. Simpson once said, it's the cause of and solution to all of life's problems.

Waylon Jennings - Sunday Morning Coming Down
Don't think of it as a hangover. Think of it as a night well spent.

—Show de Vie—

I like to think of Mike G as the documentarian that we don't deserve. His podcast is well over the 200-episode threshold and he's not slowing down at all. If you have any desire to completely nerd out on all things cocktail, subscribe to *Show de Vie*. It's practically a grad school education through an audio medium. Mike is capturing all of the stories that would disappear without him and bless him for it. I had a chance to turn the tables and do a quick interview with him having to answer the questions.

When (and how) did you start *Show de Vie?*
After a meal with a family friend in September 2015, I was regaled with these incredible stories about Hollywood and the booze industry. The gentleman had few living relatives and a son who he was at odds with. If these stories went undocumented or captured, it'd be a loss to the industry as a whole. I got the mics out of retirement and started capturing as much as possible.

Why did you decide to document this scene in this manner, and why is documentation important?
Most of our knowledge of the key personalities in this industry is through the lens of a brand. But what if instead of brand forward dialogues, we had people-focused narratives? The journeys of others are a great predictor and template for learning about our own paths. No more important resurgence of cocktail culture will occur this century, so now it's essential to capture the essence and vibrancy of the scene. It's imperative to document this era in an unfettered, unrestrained, and unfiltered way. I hope these chats serve as some kind of reference material for a great period in hospitality.

How has the Texas cocktail scene changed in the last 10 years?
All about that fresh juice. The connection to raw materials and raw
ingredients in the culinary scene has been the impetus for a shift in
cocktail culture in Texas. When you couple a keen curiosity about
terroir, construction, and production with technology, the modern era
of cocktails is all about intellectual empowerment. Both creativity
and careers behind the bar are being rewarded and acknowledged as
legitimate endeavors now. They are lucrative jobs that now assert
their place at the forefront of consumer minds in Texas. Texas went
from slinging Jack and Cokes to preparing a freshly squeezed
margarita. Once the efforts were recognized by the media and
general public, more and more people started feeling comfortable
with adventurous cocktails. The past ten years have been the age of
enlightenment with regard to food and drinks. Manhattans are a
household name now.

What makes a cocktail uniquely Texan?
I think more than any other "genre" of cocktail, Texans love to add
heat to their cocktails. Our acclimation to the Southwest cuisine and
agave spirits make them a conscious influence on how we create. Hot
summers, ubiquitous tequila—these create the perfect backdrop for
heat, acidity, and a boozy punch. We're able to deal with huge levels
of heat, frustration, and a massive population in Texas. We need a
drink that pays homage to our unique culture and tenacity. Make it
spicy and strong, we can handle it.

**What immediately comes to mind when I say the phrase "Texas
Cocktails"?**
The outdoors. Ingredients with some rusticity. Hearty and strong
willed.

PROHIBITION IN TEXAS

In the years leading up to Prohibition, Texas was becoming drier and drier. There was a very active Temperance movement in Texas, and they quickly gained support in rural areas, while the cities and the borderlands continued to be free-flowing. Eight months before the Volstead Act was signed, Texas entered into their own prohibition. In fact, Senator Morris Sheppard, from Morris County, is known as the "Father of National Prohibition," for writing the 18th Amendment. For that, we're sorry... Sidenote, during Prohibition, a still that produced 130 gallons of moonshine per day was discovered on a ranch in Texas that Sheppard owned. No wonder it was repealed fourteen years later... even the "Father of National Prohibition" didn't really mean it.

In Houston in 1927, a 600-gallon still was seized from a seven-room house built to look like a farmhouse-style shack, similar to the other small houses off Westheimer Road. The house was built for moonshining, but the windows were staged with lace curtains and fake headboards. There was a known cluster of Italian immigrants who operated a series of moonshine stills in the area. According to the *Post-Dispatch*, "246 gallons of whisky valued at $2,000 was found in one of the rooms stored in charred cypress and oak casks. A 600-gallon copper still was seized and destroyed by the officers. Other equipment included a 300-gallon cooling tank, pumps that lifted the mash from the barrels to the still, pipes that carried the refuse into a nearby cotton field and some mixing equipment." I'm secretly hoping this happened where Poison Girl is now and they find a barrel of whiskey from 1927 during the next renovation.

In Galveston, it was rum running and open era time. The period is sometimes referred to as the *open era* or the *wide-open era*, because the community made extremely little effort to hide the illegal vices. A rum row, with boats from Cuba, Jamaica, and the Bahamas, was

established 35 miles of the coast. Small boats would fetch the goods and bring them back to the Galveston shore. This was so profitable that some of the most famous rum runners, Rose and Sam Maceo, were able to open Hollywood Dinner Club, which was the most sophisticated night club on the Gulf Coast. During Prohibition the Maceos were able to gain control of Galveston's underground society, where they ran casinos, speakeasies, and night clubs. Their most famous, the Balinese Room, opened in 1929. (Be sure to check out the cocktail with the same name from Lei Low in Houston.) Not even the Great Depression was slowing Galveston down, and at one point the Maceos owned as many as sixty clubs with slot machines.

In El Paso, the border became a draw for tourists from across the United States, including politicians. In fact, in the 1920s the El Paso Chamber of Commerce found ways to promote their "Tour of Mexico," which was basically a drinking tour. Built to serve the vice

habits of Americans, Juarez boomed. A number of American distillers moved to Juarez to set up shop. Mary Dowling hired Joseph L. Beam, who was considered the best distiller in Kentucky and was suddenly out of work, to disassemble the entire Waterfill & Frazier Distillery in Kentucky and then reassemble it in Juarez, Mexico, in order to resume legal production of whiskey. Once Joseph left Juarez three years later, he went on to found a little company called Heaven Hill.

The biggest impact Prohibition had on the United States was the disappearance of spirits history. Prohibition was just long enough to destroy smaller distillers who couldn't wait for this terrible social experiment to end. It destroyed the craft. And when it was repealed, only the big guys were still standing. This lead to decade upon decade of limited American spirit options. After Prohibition, it was sixty-three years before there was a legal distillery in Texas.

MAKERS VS. FAKERS

By Mark McDavid,
Ranger Creek Brewing & Distilling

Craft distilling is exploding in the United States, which is resulting in more and more new products on the shelves at your favorite liquor stores. Some of these products are exciting, authentic, and delicious. However, if you take notice and look more closely, many of these products are inauthentic in their claims and sold under false pretenses. What you might think is a local, craft-distilled whiskey might actually be mass produced by a large industrial factory in Indiana.

This misrepresentation is happening in Texas right now. While you might see over a dozen products labeled as "Texas Whiskey" on the shelf, only a small number are actually made in Texas.

So how do you tell the makers from the fakers? When you see a spirit labeled as "Texas Whiskey," how do you know if it was actually made in Texas or sourced from out of state? While there's still not one easy answer, following these guidelines will make you an educated shopper. While Ranger Creek makes all of our Texas whiskey, we don't believe that sourcing whiskey from another company is inherently bad. The problem comes with misrepresenting sourced whiskey as hand-crafted and local. Use these guidelines to tell the difference.

1. The Label

The label is your best source for truth. Spirits labels have to be approved through the Alcohol and Tobacco Tax and Trade Bureau (TTB), a federal agency that oversees the certificates of label approval required for all spirits prior to interstate commerce. Since a federal regulator scrutinizes every word on a whiskey label, the verbiage on the label really matters. Look for the words "Distilled by." Usually it's in small print on the back. "Distilled by" means that the company actually distilled the product. If you see the words "Produced by," "Manufactured by," "Bottled by," "Filled by," "Blended by", or any others, those are red flags. The only term approved by the TTB for those that actually make their stuff is "Distilled." Although the label is your best resource, companies and regulators do sometimes make mistakes, so it's not fool proof. Look for the below phrases on a label to spot a faker or maker.

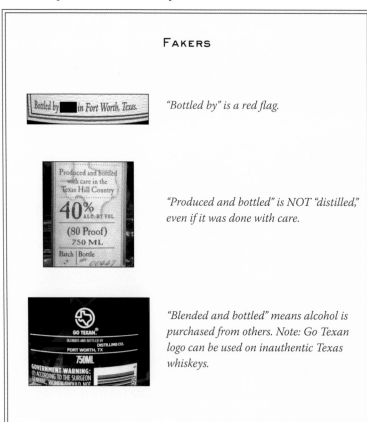

FAKERS

"Bottled by" is a red flag.

"Produced and bottled" is NOT "distilled," even if it was done with care.

"Blended and bottled" means alcohol is purchased from others. Note: Go Texan logo can be used on inauthentic Texas whiskeys.

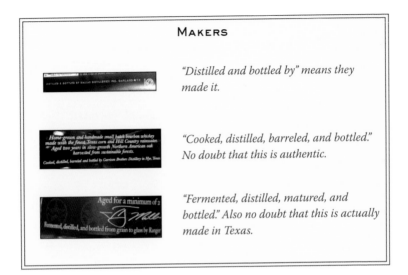

Makers

"Distilled and bottled by" means they made it.

"Cooked, distilled, barreled, and bottled." No doubt that this is authentic.

"Fermented, distilled, matured, and bottled." Also no doubt that this is actually made in Texas.

2. THE TIMELINE

If a 1–2 year old distillery is putting out a 5–6 year old whiskey, that's a HUGE red flag. It's also really common. Any new distillery that automatically has really old whiskey on the market has to be sourcing it. If you have a question, do some digging on the company's website to find out when they started distilling.

3. THE PRICE POINT

If you see a typical 750 ml bottle of Texas whiskey for $25, it's sourced. Craft distilleries are almost all new, which means we're still small. We also typically use premium ingredients and do almost everything by hand. For instance, all of the corn we use in our Texas bourbon is Texas corn. Texas corn is typically more expensive than non-Texas corn, but we're committed to using local ingredients. The economics of making craft whiskey means our stuff is generally more expensive.

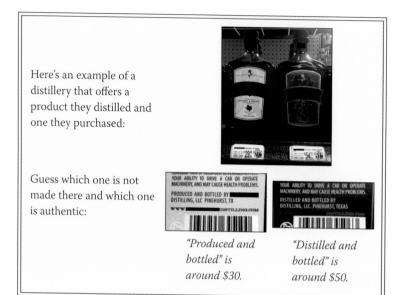

Here's an example of a distillery that offers a product they distilled and one they purchased:

Guess which one is not made there and which one is authentic:

"Produced and bottled" is around $30.

"Distilled and bottled" is around $50.

4. LIQUOR STORE EMPLOYEES

Although we have met many liquor store employees who are passionate about truth in Texas whiskey, there are often corporate policies that prevent them from communicating it to consumers. Some inauthentic whiskey brands have agreements with liquor chains that compensate them for each bottle sold. Those agreements turn into policies that require employees to push certain brands. So if you ask an average employee which Texas whiskey they recommend, you won't know if they're recommending it on their own accord or because of corporate policy.

5. DISTILLERY WEBSITES

Distillery websites and other marketing collateral are probably the worst resources for determining makers and fakers. None of this material is scrutinized through the government like labels are, so there is a lot of room for obfuscation. Fakers use images of stills and aging barrels to confuse you. Unless you read and analyze each word like a lawyer, it is very difficult to determine if they are a maker or a faker. We believe in transparency, but there is not very much of that going on right now. A few distilleries that sell sourced brands are honest about it, and whiskey drinkers commend them for their transparency.

6. OTHER INDICATORS FOR MAKERS

Many makers of true craft whiskey use unusual ingredients like oat, millet, quinoa, or, in our case, mesquite-smoked malt. The industrial manufacturers don't use these ingredients, so that's a good sign of a maker. Makers also typically brag about the fact that their whiskey is truly made from grain to glass and will brag about every step of the process being done at their distillery.

MEZCAL IN TEXAS

EMMA JANZEN, AUTHOR OF
MEZCAL: THE HISTORY, CRAFT & COCKTAILS
OF THE WORLD'S ULTIMATE ARTISANAL SPIRIT

You don't have to look much further than the ubiquitous margarita for proof that Texas has long held a deep appreciation for Mexican spirits. Tequila particularly has always had a home at the bar in the Lone Star State, so perhaps it's no surprise that Texans also quickly stepped up as early advocates for mezcal—the predecessor of tequila and godfather of Mexican spirits that

is made from various species of the agave plant—when the category started its dramatic ascent in America.

Until brands like Del Maguey, Ilegal, Sombra, and Fidencio started trickling over the border, most mezcal available in the US was of poor quality, and its reputation reflected the scorpion-laden swill in the bottle. With its inherently smoky qualities and higher-than-average proof, mezcal was considered the drunkard's choice for so long that the category didn't see much attention until pioneers like Ron Cooper and others began spreading the gospel of Mexico's most soulful spirit.

In Texas specifically, bartenders quickly realized mezcal's diverse range of flavor and mixing potential. Early adopters started stocking back bars in places like La Condesa and Takoba in Austin, Esquire

Tavern and Ocho Lounge in San Antonio, Bolsa in Dallas, and The Pastry War in Houston with better quality bottles by the case-full. In these places, where bartenders like Bobby Heugel, Alba Huerta, Jeret Peña, Eddie "Lucky" Campbell, Bill Norris, and others were creating thoughtful agave-centric menus, the spirit also naturally found a home in cocktails—one of the best introductions to the smoky, mysterious liquid for the uninitiated. Some have risen to the status of Texas icons, like Heugel's bold and unwavering The Brave from Anvil Bar & Refuge and Eaves' Texecutioner from Esquire Tavern.

Now, Texas plays home to many full-blown mezcaleria-style bars with selections that dwarf those in many other locales, like Mezcaleria Tobala and Techo in Austin, Captain Foxheart's Bad News Bar in Houston, and Dallas' Las Almas Rotas. Creative cocktails abound, and more people than ever are becoming familiar with the virtues of sip-

ping mezcal neat (with some sal de gusano on the side, of course). As long as new school brands like Mezcal Vago, El Jolgorio, Rey Campero, Real Minero, and Don Mateo continue to bring exceptional mezcal to Texas, you can be sure agave lovers will keep the momentum going strong.

TECHNOLOGY IN THE BAR

By Scott Jenkins, HIDE Bar

Innovation within the bar industry is nothing new. Bartenders tend to naturally evolve by learning and mastering classic recipes, riffing off those, and then moving on to their own concoctions. I would think it's safe to say, as it was in my case, most will make a lot of crap cocktails before they make good ones. Making great cocktails requires a few things in my opinion: curiosity and willingness to take risk; an ever-developing palette; a sensitivity and understanding of the materials you are working with; a program which provides the freedom to explore; accuracy; and a solid system for ego-checking.

I would never claim that this is the only way to approach cocktails. It is however, my preferred method. I firmly believe that cocktails (I would include food in this as well) are a language. The spirits we use have a specific history and design, an accent if you will, that gives them a certain character profile of expression. These things may seem pretentious to some, but I believe that these spirits produce a syntax used in the formation story a cocktail can tell, the story of right now. The structure of the experience one has with the cocktail right in front of them, and the perceptions which can be distinguished, give us insight into how aware of the moment we are: presentation, color, body, texture, acidity, top notes, middle notes, finishing notes, acidity, sweetness, intensity, salinity, etc. Why is this important? Because it is a direct reminder that you are alive and experiencing something. For me, this is electric and one of the reasons I am so particular about how I design and serve my cocktails.

Why Use Technology in the Bar?

Why not? Costs aside for a moment, why would you not use tools to help your craft excel? We all use bar tools, and we prefer them based off our own methodology; One can think of these as the next level extension of that tool kit. My first piece of advice for you, if you are considering using the tech below, is to not be a dick about it. NO ONE will care about your fancy equipment if you're shoving it in everyone's face as some sort of gimmick. Dispense with the theatricality that has crept its way into the scene and just put your head down and do the work. The tech is designed to allow for specific things to happen within your program, and should be left to functionality. That isn't to say that the process you used shouldn't be talked about or explained to your patrons. If they show an interest, then by all means nerd out!

Centrifuge

This is a workhorse in my program. It allows us to do many things ranging from juice clarification to blending spirits with fruit, which aids in extracting flavor without keeping the particulate from the fruit. You can purchase large units, that are refrigerated, and spin 3–4 liters of liquid at about 5000 rpm. Or, thanks to Dave Arnold of Booker and Dax, you can purchase a tabletop centrifuge which does everything a large unit can do with a different operation style. There are many resources for why these techniques are great, and you should check them out.

Rotary-Evaporator

This machine is expensive and temperamental, but cool to use. Essentially, this is a flavor scalpel, meaning you can add or strip away flavors from spirits if you know what you're doing. We use this to infuse spirits with different flavors such as habanero (the capsaicin that delivers the heat doesn't transfer), cilantro, and delicate flavors such as rose petal or chamomile. You can produce spirits that have flavors infused at the molecular level as opposed to letting product soak in the spirits for a few days. This allows for greater control over flavor expression in cocktails, and allows the product to be kept indefinitely without spoilage from oxidation or molding of leftover particulates. This rig can also be used to create essential oils, infused bitters, concentrated syrups, and hydrosols.

Carbonation

We have a system at HIDE which allows us to carbonate cocktails with tiny champagne-sized bubbles in a controlled manner. This creates a clean and crisp texture to anything we carbonate, and we test-carbonate everything we can, just because we can. If you're interested in creating your own sparkling cocktails, or sodas, take heed with this tech and research the science behind it, because carbonation is an art form.

These are just a few techniques we use at HIDE to create the most balanced, delicious, and flavorful cocktails we can dream up. There are many more techniques, machinery, and ingredients we utilize in our program, but the aforementioned should give anyone a good start at creating some truly unique experiences for their guests.

WHERE TO BUY

THE AUSTIN SHAKER
1199 AIRPORT BLVD, AUSTIN, TX 78702

When Kiki and David came to Austin from Boston, they noticed there wasn't a place they could get the "weird stuff"... combine that with a liquor store coming up for sale around the corner from their house, and the Austin Shaker was born. This is where Austin keeps their spirits weird. If they have distribution, and they're cool, odds are you'll find it here.

BAR & GARDEN
3314 ROSS AVE, STE 150, DALLAS, TX 75204

While they originally started in LA, there's only one other location, and that's in Dallas. Bar & Garden is exceedingly cool. With their mission to only sell all-natural wines and then spirits as well, Bar and Garden is like a cheat sheet for knowing who the highest quality producers are.

POGO'S WINE & SPIRITS
5360 W LOVERS LN, # 200, DALLAS, TX 75209

Harris Polakoff's family started Sigel's, Dallas' first liquor store, the day after Prohibition was lifted. In the same year they sold their family business, and Polakoff opened Pogo's, Dallas' finest independent package store, focusing on wine, liquor, cordials, and spirits.

Houston Wine Merchant
2646 S Shepherd Dr, Houston, TX 77098

Don't let the name fool you... Houston Wine Merchant has one of the best specialty spirits selections in Houston. With tasting every Friday and Saturday, they've been a catalyst in the education of the Houstonian for more than 30 years.

Pig Liquors
519 S Presa St, San Antonio, TX 78205

If they don't have it, you ain't getting it. Southtown's best is also San Antonio's. Anet Alaniz owns the best specialty liquor spot in San Antonio, and she's always helping her clients source anything she might not have in stock. This funky spot will make you smile.

Twin Liquors
Locations across Texas

Twin Liquors is probably the best of the best chain liquor stores. They're consistently knowledgeable and the selection is incredible. Born in Austin and now across the state, Twin Liquors has been a part of the Texas spirits scene for over 80 years.

TEXAS BORN, TEXAS MADE

1888 DIRTIEST MARTINI MIX

When Kenneth Hamburger wanted his martini dirtier and dirtier, he became obsessed with the way that olive juice was being used in cocktails. He decided to create an olive juice that's closer to wine than the liquid where most olives live. He uses a one-ton press to extract the juice from whole Spanish olives, and it gives you a true olive flavor with no aftertaste. If you're into dirty martinis, this is your new best friend.

ANDALUSIA WHISKEY COMPANY

Ty Phelps and Tommy Erwin, formerly of Real Ale Brewing Company, have focused their distillery on three whiskeys: the Revenant Oak, which is a peated single malt, the White Pearl, which is their white whiskey; and the Stryker, which is a smoked single malt. As these puppies age, I think they're going to start garnering national recognition. Watch out for these dudes.

BLOODY REVOLUTION

Genuinely, some of the best Bloody Mary mixers I've had come from Austin. Longtime friends Chantz Hoover and Greg Bodle decided that their favorite drink, the Bloody Mary, deserved as much of a craft treatment as the rest of the cocktails out there, and they made Bloody Revolution. With six flavors, each provides a different, but delicious, way to approach your favorite brunch cocktail. And the Ribeye flavor is basically steak in a glass, which doesn't suck in the slightest.

Elk Store Winery & Distillery

Czech brothers Todd Smajstrla and Scott Hladky are carrying on their family tradition of moonshining at this Fredricksburg distillery. And yes, the majority of great-grand-daddy's moonshining did come during Prohibition. You'll have to visit Elk Store to try their selection of spirits including pecan pie moonshine, oak-infused moonshine, white rum, and old tom gin, to name a few. They are not distributed, but if you find yourself in wine country, go have yourself a moonshine.

Martine Honeysuckle Liqueur

I remember as a kid being at my abuelita's house smelling, picking, and sucking the nectar out of honeysuckle right off the plant. Honeysuckle plays a role in almost every Texan's childhood at some point. Gary Kelleher, the co-founder of Dripping Springs Vodka, spent five years perfecting his honeysuckle liqueur recipe. Kelleher wanted Martine to not only taste like a honeysuckle in blossom, but to also capture the aroma of the flower. Martine does both, beautifully.

Monjus Spirits

The Monju story involves a 19th century move from the Balearic Islands in Spain to New Orleans, continues with a distilling operation on Burgundy Street in the French Quarter, and begins again with finding an ancient family recipe book. Monju is just starting, but they're one of the products I'm most looking forward to. They make several varieties of Spanish-grape-based absinthes and are definitely one to watch.

On the Rocks Cocktails

After Rocco Milano left The Mansion in Dallas, he headed up the programs at Private Social and Barter. Having spent his career creating flavor combinations, he wanted to move into distilling. As one will do, he needed a way to make money without waiting on product to age, so Rocco began creating bottled cocktail recipes. On the Rocks cocktails are some of the most delicious, ready-to-drink cocktails out there.

Paula's Texas Spirits

Paula Angerstein received the second distiller's license in Texas, after Tito, in 2003 and launched Paula's Texas Orange and Paula's Texas Lemon. Her flavors are based on more of a limoncello style than typical orange liqueurs and are usually around twice the proof. Paula was one of the first female distillers in the United States, and her products can be found in bars and on menus arcoss the state.

Railean American Made Rum

Railean started in 2005 when Kelly Railean quit her corporate job and started to champion the very spirit that fueled the American revolution. Located in San Leon, on the shores of Galveston Bay with all of the history of rum running in that part of the world, it seem appropriate that Railean was the first woman-owned distillery to make American rum.

Witherspoon Distilling

Quentin Witherspoon, one of the founders and the brand's namesake, taught himself how to distill while in Bangui, the capital of the Central African Republic where he was on assignment to protect some American diplomats. Witherspoon was in charge of filtering their drinking water from the Congo. As the group's goods began to spoil, he began to distill wine into brandy and then beer into whiskey. Quentin now has his own distillery in Lewisville and is producing a single malt and a straight bourbon whiskey.

CLASSIC
Cocktails

★ ★

**"YOU MAY ALL GO TO HELL
AND I WILL GO TO TEXAS."**

—Davy Crockett

We don't have a lot of classic cocktail history that originated from the Lone Star State. In fact, the two "classics" that absolutely came from here are both pretty micro regional in nature, but both quite popular across Texas now. Now, if you order them in Denver on the other hand, you may get a blank stare. However, there are plenty of quintessential Texas drinks that have formed the cocktail culture as we know it. Margaritas, Palomas, even the dreaded and feared Mexican Martini, have all provided the foundation of the Texas cocktail movement, and for that reason, you better know how to make a frozen margarita...

★ ★

⟶ CHILTON ⟵

The Chilton is one of the two "classic" cocktails that can be attributed to Texas. According to members of the Lubbock Country Club, a local doctor, Dr. Chilton to be exact, asked his bartender to mix the juice of two lemons with vodka and soda and serve it over ice, with a salt rim. Ta-dah! Chilton! It's a sunny and dry panhandle day in a glass. That's one thing about these West Texas cocktails… they're always as dry as the land they come from.

Glassware: **Highball Glass**
Garnish: **Lemon Wheel**

- **1.5 oz Texas vodka (try Dripping Springs or Cinco)**
- **Juice of 2 lemons**
- **Topo Chico**

1. Rim a highball glass with salt, then fill it with ice.

2. Add vodka and lemon juice, then top with Topo Chico and stir.

3. Garnish with a lemon wheel.

~ FROZEN MARGARITA ~

In Dallas in 1971, Mariano Martinez had a problem. Too many people wanted margaritas and it was taking too long to make them. After a sleepless night, Mariano stopped by a convenience store on the way to work for coffee, saw a slushie machine, and the rest is history. Soon, he was making margaritas in a soft-serve ice-cream machine, and he called it "The World's First Frozen Margarita Machine." Over time, the frozen margarita has undoubtedly become the most popular cocktail in the entire state of Texas. When I sat down with Bobby Heugel, I asked which cocktail was the quintessential Texas cocktail and he responded, "A frozen margarita. They serve them at every tex-mex place in the state and it's the drink that we were given sips of as kids. It's the frozen margarita, definitely."

Glassware: **Margarita Glass or Frozen Mug**
Garnish: **Lime Wedge**

- **2 oz blanco tequila**
- **1 oz fresh lime juice**
- **.75 oz Cointreau**

1. Add tequila, lime juice and Cointreau along with 1 cup of ice to your blender. Blend until smooth.

2. Pour into a chilled, salted margarita glass or frozen mug.

3. Garnish with a lime wheel.

David Alan (Tipsy Texan) believes that "the drink is essentially a margarita presented in a cocktail shaker and then poured tableside into a cocktail glass rimmed with salt and garnished with a jalapeño-stuffed olive. At its worst it is shaken with Rose's lime juice or other adulterants." I completely agree. So if I was to try to make my own Mexican Martini, this is the recipe I'd go with.

MEXICAN MARTINI

Oh the Mexican Martini ... so popular in Texas, yet so bizarre. I felt the need to include this based solely on its meteoric rise in popularity in Texas (specifically Austin) and the fact that, odds are, someone behind the bar will be able to make it. There's debate as to where the drink originated and which approach is best, but I will say that if you're going to wade into the waters of the Mexican Martini, leave the Sprite and orange juice at home. This is two drinks, and two strong ones at that. Consume only on a patio with chips, salsa, queso, and guacamole on the table, preferably while waiting for the fajitas to finish grilling.

Glassware: **Martini Glass**
Garnish: **Jalapeño-Stuffed Olive**

- **3 oz reposado tequila**
- **1.5 oz Cointreau**
- **1.5 oz fresh lime juice**
- **.5 oz 1888 Dirtiest Martini Mix**

1. Combine ingredients in a shaker with ice and shake vigorously.

2. Strain into a chilled martini glass, rimmed with salt.

3. Leave remaining cocktail in the shaker and refill glass as needed.

~ PALOMA ~

The history of this drink is unclear; however, credit is usually given to Don Javier Delgado Corona from the La Capilla bar in Jalisco, Mexico, and it's said that he might have named it after a folk song from the 1860s called "La Paloma." Margaritas have taken over the United States, but in Mexico, where the tequila comes from, it's the Paloma. The first case in print is rumored to be by Evan Harrison who wrote *Popular Cocktails of The Rio Grande.* Traditionally, this cocktail includes grapefruit soda, like Jarritos, but I prefer it with fresh grapefruit and Topo Chico. I mean, when you have some of the best in the world, why would you not?

Glassware: **Collins Glass**
Garnish: **Grapefruit slice**

- **1 oz fresh grapefruit juice**
- **.5 oz fresh lime juice**
- **.5 oz agave nectar**
- **1.5 oz blanco tequila**
- **Topo Chico**

1. Combine ingredients, except Topo Chico, in a shaker with ice and shake vigorously.

2. Strain into a collins glass with ice. Top with Topo Chico.

3. Garnish with a grapefruit slice.

~ RANCH WATER ~

Ranch Water has a bit of a cult cocktail. This uniquely West Texas drink is rumored to have started in the 1960s. The Gage Hotel in Marathon, after years of making the drink for those requesting it, made it official by putting the drink on the menu in 2010. It's the epitome of simplicity and you can sip on them all day. It's the tequila-based equivalent of the light beer you drink while working in the yard or lounging by the river. Plenty of bars in Texas that have tried to fancy or sweeten up the Ranch Water by adding simple syrup or clarifying lime juice or even swapping the tequila for a different agave spirit, but simplicity is best, my friends.

Glassware: **Topo Chico**
Garnish: **Lime Wedge**

---

* **12 oz bottle of Topo Chico**
* **1.5 oz blanco tequila**
* **.25 oz fresh lime juice**

1. Start by pouring out two ounces of the Topo Chico.

2. Add the tequila and lime juice to the Topo Chico bottle.

3. Garnish with lime wedge.

~ TEXAS FIZZ ~

The Texas Fizz ain't from Texas y'all. Two London-based bartenders first published this cocktail recipe in 1922, smack dab in the middle of Prohibition, meaning the citizens of this cocktail's namesake couldn't even have one! Originally the recipe called for seltzer, but in 1936 Frank Meier of the Ritz Hotel in Paris published a recipe replacing the seltzer with champagne to kick it up a notch. And rightfully so… I mean, if you're going to use our name, it needs to be a little more interesting than gin, juice, and seltzer.

Glassware: **Collins Glass**
Garnish: **Orange Twist**

- **1.5 oz London dry gin**
- **.5 oz fresh lemon juice**
- **.75 oz fresh orange juice**
- **.25 oz grenadine**
- **2–3 oz chilled brut champagne**

1. Combine ingredients in a shaker with ice and shake vigorously.

2. Strain into a chilled collins glass and top with champagne.

— TOMMY'S MARGARITA —

If you're going to do a margarita, do Tommy's Margarita bypass the orange liqueur and hit it with agave. This version of the margarita was created by Julio Bermejo at Tommy's Mexican Restaurant in San Francisco in the 1990s. This is simply the freshest approach to a simple margarita. Memorize this one.

Glassware: **Margarita Glass**
Garnish: **Salt, for rimming (optional), and Lime Wedge**

- **2 oz tequila, 100% agave**
- **1 oz lime juice**
- **.5 oz agave nectar**

1. Combine ingredients in a shaker with ice and shake vigorously.

2. Strain into a margarita glass, rimmed with salt.

3. Garnish with lime wedge.

CREATIVE
Concoctions

★ ★

"IF YOU'RE JUST GOING TO DO WHAT EVERYBODY ELSE HAS DONE BEFORE, WHO CARES?"

— Chip Tate

Charlotte Voisey from William Grant & Sons once told me that working behind a bar is, simply, theatre. I wholeheartedly agree. I'd also add a bit of science and you have the makings of some awfully creative concoctions. Of course, when you go to a bar like The Aviary in Chicago or Dandelyan in London, you'll see some of the most imaginative uses of technology in the cocktail world but because of the way that information spreads nowadays, these ideas are migrating.

In Texas, while we're certainly laidback in our approach to most of life, we can execute a cocktail with the expertise and precision of the best bartenders in the world. This chapter has a few examples of some of the inventive approaches you can find in this rapidly advancing cocktail community. These are cocktails that you should absolutely try to make at home... if you have all of the stuff to do so and don't mind diving down the rabbit hole a bit.

★ ★

~ LANDRACE ~

Esquire Tavern Downstairs
Recipe: Myles Worrell, Downstairs, 2016
155 E Commerce St
San Antonio, TX 78205
(210) 222-2521

esquiretavern-sa.com/downstairs

Okay, so … here's a little secret … there's a speakeasy inside a cocktail bar in San Antonio. Meta, I know. But the Downstairs at Esquire Tavern is truly a different world from the raucous party happening above. With Hank Cathey coming up with some of the most innovative drinks and drink presentations in the city, Downstairs is an experience in and of its own. With an entrance on the Riverwalk itself, Downstairs is an intimate lounge dishing out "unconventional inclinations." This place is nice. I'm talking really nice. This isn't a cocktail dive bar… this is, unquestionably, the nicest bar on the Riverwalk and the drinks are absolutely incredible.

Glassware: **Cocktail Glass**
Garnish: **Orange Twist**

- 2 oz Blue Corn gin
- 1 oz Huitlachoche vermouth
- 1 oz Luxardo maraschino liqueur
- 1 dash Regan's orange bitters
- 1 dash Bittermens Scarborough bitters

1. Stir all ingredients well with ice in a mixing glass, and strain into a chilled cocktail glass.

2. Express oil from a large swath of orange peel over the drink, and garnish with an orange twist.

BLUE CORN GIN

- 8 oz landrace Mexican blue corn
- 1L Greenall's gin

Combine. Macerate for 14 days. Agitate daily.

HUITLACHOCHE TINCTURE

- 32 oz Huitlachoche
- 32 oz Everclear

Combine. Macerate for 24 hours. Fine strain.

HUITLACHOCHE VERMOUTH

- 5 parts Boisserre dry vermouth
- 1 part Huitlachoche tincture

Combine all ingredients.

— THE LITTLEJOHN COBBLER —

Daiquiri Time Out
Recipe: Brad Stringer
2701 Market St
Galveston, TX 77550
(409) 497-2760

dtogalveston.com

I couldn't be happier that Texas has a bar named DTO (Daiquiri Time Out). I also couldn't be happier that it's Brad Stringer at the helm. First at Boheme, then Johnny's Gold Brick in Houston, now he leads Galveston into craft cocktail culture with seasonal menus and a variety of styles for guests to consume. The Littlejohn Cobbler takes its name from Elbridge Gerry Littlejohn (1862–1935), who was one of the great documentarians of South Texas and the author of *Texas History Stories* and *Geography of Texas*. At DTO, the kumquats used in this cocktail typically come from the property where Littlejohn built his home.

Glassware: **Julep Mug**
Garnish: **Mint Sprig, Sliced Strawberry, Sliced Kumquat, Powdered Sugar**

- **1.5 oz Kumquat-Strawberry Syrup**
- **.75 oz PX sherry**
- **.75 oz Oloroso sherry**
- **.75 oz Plantation OFTD rum**
- **.25 oz fresh lime juice**

1. Combine ingredients in a shaker with ice and shake vigorously, then strain over ice in julep mug.

2. Top with crushed ice.

3. Garnish with mint sprig, sliced strawberry, sliced kumquat, and powdered sugar.

KUMQUAT-
STRAWBERRY
CORDIAL

- 1 cup fresh kumquat juice
- 3 cups strawberry syrup
- .75 cup vodka

Cut and macerate
strawberries in sugar to
make strawberry syrup.

—Moving Sidewalk—

306 MAIN ST
HOUSTON, TX 77002
MOVINGSIDEWALKBAR.COM

Moving Sidewalk's Alex Gregg, known for his unique and sometimes obsessive approach to drinks, developed a recipe for the cocktail that fits the style of his Houston Bar, Moving Sidewalk. Alex first clarified and carbonated a standard Screwdriver (vodka and orange juice) with a few tweaks to the acidity. From there the Screwdriver component is placed on a draft system and dispensed into collins glass with ice. It is then topped with a foam made from Galliano and aquafaba (chickpea water) using an ISI whipped cream canister.

~ ADVANCED HARVEY ~ WALLBANGER

Recipe: Alex Gregg

Glassware: **Collins Glass**
Garnish: **Dehydrated half orange wheel**

- 1.5 parts citrus vodka
- 1.5 parts clarified orange juice
- .5 parts House Lemon Cordial
- .5 parts House Lime Cordial
- .25 parts Citric Acid Solution (4%)

Combine all in a cornelius keg and carbonate with a 10 micro carbonation stone at 50 psi for 2 days. Pour draft cocktail into an ice-filled collins glass. Garnish with a dehydrated half orange wheel.

GALLIANO FOAM

- 1 part Galliano
- 1.5 parts aquafaba (chickpea water)
- .75 parts simple syrup (2:1)
- Charged in ISI whipper, with 2 Cream (Nitro) chargers.

CLARIFIED ORANGE JUICE

- 2 grams of Agar Agar
- 1 L orange juice

Carefully measure Agar Agar and juice and combine in a pot. Slowly bring to a boil, then simmer for 2 minutes. Remove from heat and transfer to a hotel pan. This mixture will set like Jello. Once set, place the pan into a freezer to freeze overnight. Once frozen, transfer the raft to a perforated hotel pan lined with cheesecloth and place in a refrigerator. The frozen raft will slowly drip as it melts, yielding clarified juice.

HOUSE LEMON AND LIME CORDIALS

- 2 parts lemon juice
- 1 part simple syrup

Combine juice and syrup, then follow the process for clarifying juice. The resulting cordial will be shelf stable for weeks.

CITRIC ACID SOLUTION

- 4 grams food grade citric acid
- 96 grams filtered water

Combine all ingredients and stir.

AQUAFABA

This is chickpea water; and you can make your own by soaking fresh chickpeas in water, or, alternatively, use the water from canned chickpeas.

THYME/CITRUS WATER:

Boil 2 liters water with 8 ounces thyme, 8 ounces brown sugar, and the zest from 2 limes.

Then strain that and mix with:

- 10 oz fresh orange juice
- 8 oz grapefruit juice
- 12 oz lemon juice
- 16 oz lime juice

Neighborhood Services
Recipe: Ivan J Rimach
5027 W Lovers Lane
Dallas, TX 75209
(214) 350-5027

nhstheoriginal.com

Neighborhood Services is one of the most important institutions in Dallas culinary history. Having multiple locations, one of the biggest influences was the Neighborhood Services Tavern, which was run by famed bartender Jason Kosmas shortly after moving to Dallas. Many a Dallasite has been introduced to cocktails by Jason at Neighborhood Services (including myself), and in a manner similar to the food served, the Neighborhood Service cocktail program has always been about approachability. This cocktail is a simple riff on a pisco sour and is mighty delicious, y'all.

Glassware: **Rocks Glass**
Garnish: **Lemon Wheel, Thyme Sprig**

- .75 oz lime juice
- .5 oz simple syrup
- .75 oz Thyme/Citrus Water
- 2 oz Pisco Cuatro G's Acholado
- Ginger beer

1. Add all ingredients to a rocks glass and stir.

2. Top with ginger beer.

—Caffe Del Fuego—

RFDISTILLERS.COM

Caffe Del Fuego is one of the most pleasant surprises of this journey. This is a coffee lover's dream spirit. It's a five-bean blend of Arabica coffee beans from micro lot farms in Brazil, El Salvador, Mexico, Ethiopia, and Indonesia that contribute to these specialty grade coffees. They work hand-in-hand with the Austin Roasting Company in creating the blend.

The Fuego guys then heat-brew this freshly roasted and ground coffee at a very proper 202 degrees, and then add pure cane dark sugar and Madagascar bourbon vanilla.

They're the only coffee liquor that uses this method, which is significant because there are 150 flavonoids in heat-brewed coffee and only 25 in cold-brewed coffee. IF you've ever compared cold-brew directly to the same beans heat-brewed, you know what I'm talking about.

Fuego is a delicious, alcoholic, caffeinated coffee... which makes it perfect for day drinking. Frankly, as I write this, I'm enjoying my "Saturday morning coffee" right now, because, 3 oz of Fuego has about 40 mg of caffeine.

When I asked about mixing Fuego into a cocktail, founder Peter Remington told me, "While Fuego is killer in any cocktail that currently uses another brand of coffee liqueur (and, trust me, we've sipped a lot of them) we love it on the rocks. Done. It is the ultimate Adult Iced Coffee. And if you have a sweet tooth, just add a little splash of half and half. Boom. Adult Iced Latte." Sounds magical, huh?

Founded in Austin, Texas, in 2013 by cousins Peter and Mark Remington Koelsch, their first spirit is Caffe del Fuego. The name loosely means "coffee of the fire" or "fire coffee" and is an intentional hybrid of Italian and Spanish. Caffe del Fuego is based on a recipe shared by an old Italian gentleman and friend named Vincent who agreed to the use of the recipe with one rule: Don't screw it up.

Vincent, my man... they didn't.

THE SOUTH TEXAN

* 1 oz Caffe del Fuego
* 1 oz quality Anejo
* .25 oz quality orange liqueur
* .125 oz Ancho Reyes
* 2 dashes orange bitters
* 2 dashes chocolate bitters

On the rocks, stirred, and garnished with an orange peel.

～ BERRY WHITE ～

Recipe: Devin McCullough, The People's Last Stand

The Berry White is especially tasty if you're looking for a kick of bourbon, but it's still refreshing and not overly boozy.

Glassware: **Red or White Stemless Wine Glass**
Garnish: **Berry Compote, Long Lemon Peel with Bamboo Pick**

- **2 oz bourbon (4 Roses or Old Grand Dad)**
- **.75 oz fresh orange juice**
- **.5 oz fresh lemon juice**
- **.5 oz rich demerara syrup**
- **1 oz Wild Berry Cordial**

1. Combine ingredients in a shaker with ice and shake vigorously.

2. Double strain into wine glass.

3. Top with berry composte and garnish with lemon peel.

Wild Berry Cordial

- **2 pints blueberries**
- **1 pint blackberries**
- **1 pint raspberries**
- **1.5 pints brown sugar**
- **8 oz bourbon (4 Roses or Old Grand Dad)**

Cook to a boil or when the berries start to pop.

Chill cordial. Then double strain into a glass bottle.

Berry Compote

Soak wild berries in cognac.

—The People's Last Stand—

5319 E MOCKINGBIRD LN
DALLAS, TX 75206
(214) 370-8755
THEPEOPLESLASTSTAND.COM

One of the first cocktail-centric programs in Dallas, People's Last Stand is an island of cool in the sea of suburban-esque Mockingbird Station. With alumni like Alex Fletcher (Atwater Alley), Omar Yeefoon (Shoals Sound and Service), Chris Dempsey (D & D Shrubs and Strups), and others, People's Last Stand has played a pivotal role in the ascension of cocktails in Dallas.

~ PAJARO DEL FUEGO ~

King Bee
Recipe: Billy Hankey
1906 E 12th St
Austin, TX 78702
(512) 600-6956

King Bee took over for the Legendary White Swan in 2014, and while the spot is much more bar than venue, they still host a Blues Night residency on Mondays. The proprietors, Billy and Colette, are two of the sweetest, kindest people you'll ever meet. Colette slinging some incredible pizza and Billy doing the same with drinks, King Bee is everything you'd want in a neighborhood bar. Don't shy away from this cocktail because you have to make a shrub. Just make plenty and throw it in the refrigerator. Shrubs will last up to a month and they're an incredibly easy way to put a quick cocktail together.

Glassware: **Collins Glass**
Garnish: **Lime Wedge**

- 1.5 oz Caffe del Fuego
- 1.5 oz pineapple shrub
- .75 oz Campari
- .75 oz lime juice

1. Combine ingredients in a shaker with ice and shake vigorously.

2. Strain into a collins glass, over fresh cubed ice.

3. Garnish with a lime wedge.

PINEAPPLE SHRUB

- 1 medium pineapple, sliced (including peels and core)
- 1.3 cups demerara sugar
- .5 cup white wine vinegar
- .5 cup apple cider vinegar
- Wooden spoon
- Large stainless steel bain marie
- Immersion blender
- Cutting board
- Sharp, large knife

1. Wash the pineapple and remove the top. Cut up the pineapple into manageable pieces, including the core and the skin. Add the pineapple to the bainmarie, keeping as much juice as possible. Mix in the Demerara sugar with a wooden spoon, and allow mixture to sit at room temperature for about 30 minutes.

2. Mix again, and ensure that the sugars have begun to pull the juice out of the pineapple skin and fruit. Then add the white wine vinegar and the apple cider vinegar. If an immersion blender is available, use the blender in short bursts to break apart any of the larger chunks of pineapple. Cover the mixture with plastic wrap, or a lid, and allow the mixture to sit in a cooler for about 48 hours, stirring 2–3 times daily.

★ ★

"HOUSTON'S ONE OF THE MOST DIVERSE URBAN AREAS IN THE ENTIRE COUNTRY, AND MOST PEOPLE HERE ARE REALLY PROUD OF THAT."

—Laura Moser

Everyone who's into cocktails in Texas owes a lot to Bobby Heugel. The story of Anvil Bar & Refuge is well documented. From being the first cocktail bar in Texas to creating the list of 100 cocktails that everyone should try, the evolution of their training program is jokingly referred to as "The University." Anvil is the cornerstone of Texas cocktails. Were people doing it before Anvil? Yep... but that has never been the most important thing about it. It's the structure, the attention to detail, and the fact that it was the spark that started the wildfire that cocktails have become that makes Anvil influential.

Houston has become a destination for some of the best drink makers in the world. The creativity and ingenuity shown in Houston is on par with any scene, anywhere. Houston is one of the top culinary cities in America, and, without a doubt, their cocktail history has played a vital role in their ascent. The fusion of cultures in Houston resonates strongly in the way they go about making drinks. As one of the largest, most diverse cities in America, Houston's cocktail scene is a direct reflection of itself.

While writing this, Hurricane Harvey hit and its impact will be felt from now on. Forever. The estimated cost of the storm is $190 billion. Yes, with a *b*. But we'll recover. Houston will recover. Rockport will recover. Victoria, Port Aransas, Port Arthur, and Conroe will all recover. That's how we're built. Texans are the most resilient people I know. If there's devastation, we bond together. If there's tragedy, we are the support system. If there's anywhere in the world that can take a catastrophic event like Hurricane Harvey and turn it into a rally for a community, it's Texas.

Houston Strong.

★ ★

—Anvil Bar & Refuge—

1424 WESTHEIMER RD
HOUSTON, TX 77006
(713) 523-1622
ANVILHOUSTON.COM

The quality of bars in the state is directly proportional to the expectation established by our first one, Anvil Bar & Refuge. Anvil has been nominated for or won basically everything from Spirited Awards to local media awards to consistently ranking in World's Best Bars... and throw in being a semifinalist for the James Beard Award for Outstanding Bar Program. This is, without question, the most intense, knowledge-filled training program I've ever seen. Some of those who have made their way through the program literally refer to it as The University. This is grad school, y'all.

Recipe: Terry Williams

Anvil Bar & Refuge is dedicated to making the best drinks they can with the highest quality spirits and ingredients they can find. Their dedication to specificity is world-class. This is the best bar in Texas.

Glassware: **Rocks Glass**
Garnish: **Grated Cinnamon, Cinnamon Stick**

- **1.5 oz Old Granddad BIB bourbon**
- **.5 oz Cocchi Torino vermouth**
- **.5 oz Lustau East India sherry**
- **.5 oz Salers Gentiane**
- **1 barspoon turbinado syrup**
- **1 dash Angostura bitters**
- **1 dash Bittermen's mole bitters**

Stir all ingredients and strain over ice. Grate cinnamon on top and garnish with a cinnamon stick.

~ THE BARRINGER ~

Barringer Bar & Lounge
Recipe: Chieko & Robby Cook
108 Main St
Houston, TX 77002
(832) 786-1836

barringerhouston.com

Run by the husband and wife team of Robby and Chieko Cook, Barringer Bar & Lounge takes its name from the old Barringer Norton Tailors, where the bar originally resided. The bar has an intimate, warm vibe, and the Texans running the bar couldn't be more hospitable. The bar's namesake cocktail is a great twist on a daisy.

Glassware: **Coupe Glass**
Garnish: **Lemon Wheel**

- 1.5 oz whiskey (we try to use Texas brands like TX Whiskey, but it tastes great with any)
- .75 oz dry curacao (Pierre Ferrand)
- .5 oz turbinado simple syrup
- .5 oz fresh lemon juice

1. Combine ingredients in a shaker with ice and shake vigorously.

2. Fine strain into a coupe glass.

3. Garnish with a lemon wheel.

WHITMEYER'S
— TEXAS —
PEACH
FLAVORED
WHISKEY

Handcrafted in small batches

750 mL

40% Alc./Vol. (80 Proof)

—Whitmeyer's Distilling—

Back in 2003, while stationed in Germany with the US Army, Travis Whitmeyer met a girl whose family had been making alcohol for generations. "When I was stationed in Germany, I started dating one of the local girls there. She invited me over for supper one evening and being a good diplomat, I brought them some Hershey's chocolate and a case of Budweiser. They loved the chocolate and hated the beer," Travis said. They lived on a small Bavarian farm, and turned their surplus produce into various beers, wines, ciders, and schnapps. Travis couldn't get enough of it and decided to study their process.

Once he returned to the US from his tour of duty, Travis started going to the University of Houston. His brother Chris, who was also an Iraq veteran, started attending Lamar University. Travis said, "One of my first business classes, I had to write a business plan, so I wrote one for a distillery. Thirteen years later, here we are." Travis convinced his dad and brother to join him and they wound up raising money from friends and family to start. Whitmeyer's Distilling opened the first legal distillery in Harris County in 2012. Their products are available across the state.

~ THE COLT .45 ~

Whitmeyer's Distilling
16711 Hollister St
Houston, TX 77066
(713) 623-1637
whitmeyers.com

This is a fun, coffee filled twist on an Old Fashioned. It will pep you up and get you going at the same time!

Glassware: **Rocks Glass**
Garnish: **Orange Twist**

- 2 oz Whitmeyer's Texas bourbon
- .5 oz coffee liquor
- 2 dashes of orange bitters

Stir all ingredients and garnish with an orange twist.

WHITMEYER'S

— TEXAS —

SINGLE
BARREL

CASK STRENGTH

Straight Bourbon Whiskey

— 750 mL —

56% Alc./Vol. (112 Proof)

Better Luck Tomorrow
Recipe: Alex Negranza
544 Yale St
Houston, TX 77007
(713) 802-0845
betterlucktomorrowhou.com

Better Luck Tomorrow is a neighborhood bar with restaurant-quality food from James Beard Award winner Justin Yu. (The party melt is one of the best burger-like sandwiches I've ever had.) Set in The Heights in Houston, Better Luck Tomorrow is a neighborhood bar with incredible food and stellar drinks. This is what the cocktail scene is moving to and it's one of the best things that could happen for the democratization of cocktails. There's been a shift in the restaurant industry away from "a restaurant with great drinks" to "a bar with great food," and BLT is a prime example. There's no 100 list here, even though your bartender will be able to make anything off of it, but there is special attention paid to the affordability and accessibility of the cocktail menu.

Glassware: **Libbey Coupe Glass**
Garnish: **Red Vein Sorrel Leaf**

- 1.5 oz Krogstad aquavit
- .5 oz lime juice
- .5 oz orgeat syrup
- 1 egg white
- 1 french sorrel leaf

1. Combine ingredients in a shaker with ice and shake vigorously.

2. Fine strain into a coupe glass.

Johnny's Gold Brick
2518 Yale St
Houston, TX 77008
(713) 864-2424

treadsack.com/johnnys

This recipe may seem a little daunting, but it's one of the most straightforward concepts you'll find in bars. It's a shot and a beer. The beautiful thing about this recipe is that you're making a batched old fashioned, which in and of itself can be fun to play around with. (Try getting one of those tiny barrels and aging it a bit.) Just make sure you double the amount of water, then pour over ice and garnish with orange zest and a cherry. Johnny's Gold Brick, to me, is a quintessential Texas cocktail bar. When you walk in you'll see the doctor who lives around the corner, the mechanic just off work, and everyone in between. And odds are they're both drinking boilermakers... at least for the first round. And you'll have plenty since this recipe is for about 50 ounces.

Glassware: **Shot Glass**
Garnish: **Salt, Sugar, Orange Slice**

- **32 oz Mellow Corn Whiskey (any inexpensive whiskey, the higher the proof the better, 90–100 proof for best results)**
- **10 oz purified water**
- **8 oz orange cherry syrup**
- **1 oz Angostura bitters**

1. Combine all ingredients and mix thoroughly. Bottle in a resealable bottle and refrigerate for up to one month. Serve chilled.

2. Serve in a shot glass rimmed with a combination of salt and sugar in the raw and an orange slice soaked in Angostura bitters.

3. Accompany the shot with a Lone Star beer.

ORANGE CHERRY SYRUP

- 8 oz cherry syrup from Luxardo or Armerena Cherries (the syrup is in the jar or can that the cherries themselves come in).
- 1 whole orange (peels only)

Bring cherry syrup and peels to a light simmer, remove from heat immediately, and let cool with the peels in the syrup. If you boil the syrup with the peels it will become bitter.

Strain out the peels and store in an airtight container for up to one month.

~ WHAT REALLY HAPPENED ~

Recipe: Erik Bogle, Houston Watch Company

Asimultaneously playful and reverent tribute to one of Houston's strongest, fiercest, most independent, and successful women. When asked to describe the cocktail, head barman Erik Bogel said "I was inspired by a raw and emotional artistic journey that made intense personal revelations public by way of some of the most bangin' tracks to come out of our fair city. The ingredients represent my interpretation of the story, but like any art, you're free to assign your own meanings."

The drink itself is a bright refreshing palate cleanser. A sunny day sipper that might remind you that a little self-reflection on a hot sunny day in Texas can put you in the mindset to be powerful and achieve greatness.

Glassware: **Collins Glass**
Garnish: **Lemon Peel**

- .75 oz London dry gin
- .75 oz Barrow's Intense Ginger liqueur
- .75 oz lemon juice
- .25 oz honey syrup

1. Combine ingredients in a shaker with ice and shake vigorously.

2. Dump container along with shaken (now cracked) ice into a collins glass.

3. Express oils by squeezing, then garnish with lemon peel.

Houston Watch Co.'s honey syrup is made by adding
64% water by weight to standard clover honey.

—Houston Watch Co.—

913 FRANKLIN ST
HOUSTON, TX 77002
(713) 485-0006
HOUSTONWATCHCOMPANY.COM

The Houston Watch Company is located in the Southern Pacific Railroad Building, which was built in 1910. In 1912, Houston jeweler V. A. Corrigan opened his Houston Watch Company in the Franklin Street retail space adjacent to the building's lobby. Today, it's where you can find some of the best drinks in the city in a relaxed atmosphere presented with impeccable service.

—Lei Low—

6412 N MAIN ST
HOUSTON, TX 77009
(713) 380-2968
LEILOWHTX.COM

"You're going to Lei Low?"
"Yeah…"
"Be careful man… You'll love it. It's an incredible time… but we call it getting 'Lei Low'd' around here for a reason."

Lei Low is a neighborhood tiki bar in a strip mall by a tire shop… and once you've been, you may never end your night at a different bar again. Russell loves tiki drinks and honestly, all he wants is for you to love them too. I asked him about the genesis of the Balinese Room #2 and he said "It was named for the Famous Galveston nightclub (and ZZ Top song) the Balinese Room. Growing up in Houston, one spends a lot of time in Galveston. One of Galveston's most famous or even infamous Polynesian Sites was the Balinese Room. It was owned by Bootlegger and Mafia Types and served as a speakeasy, illegal casino, and Supper Club to the rich and famous people in the area."

~ BALINESE ROOM #2 ~

Lei Low

Why #2? Russell Theode said, "It's #2 because a friend of mine, Alex Gregg of Moving Sidewalk, created another cocktail with the same name, so like in an old cocktail book it's #2."

Glassware: **Absinthe Rinsed Chilled Daiquiri Glass**
Garnish: **Lime Wedge, Star Anise**

- 1 oz Plantation Grande Reserve Barbados 5yr
- 1 oz Dimmi Apertif
- 1 oz yellow chartreuse
- 1 oz fresh lime juice
- 1 dash Angostura bitters

1. Combine ingredients in a shaker with ice and shake vigorously.

2. Fine strain into an absinthe rinsed, chilled daiquiri glass.

3. Garnish with lime and star anise.

Marriott Marquis
Recipe: Nathan Reffell
1777 Walker St
Houston, TX 77010
(713) 654-1777

http://www.marriottmarquishouston.com/

Nathan Reffell is one of my favorite people on the planet. The vice president of the Houston chapter of the USBG is overseeing the menu at one of the coolest places in the city, especially over the summer. Perched on the sixth-floor of Parkview Terrace, High Dive serves handcrafted cocktails in a resort-like atmosphere. It has killer views with even better drinks. Bonus, this cocktail helped Nate become a finalist in the 2017 Star of the Bar competition.

Glassware: **Coupe Glass**

- 2 oz Hendrinks
- .75 oz aperol
- .75 oz lemon juice
- .5 oz simple syrup
- Muddled red bell pepper
- Pinch of black pepper

1. Combine ingredients in a shaker with ice and shake vigorously.

2. Strain into a coupe glass.

3. Add black pepper and serve.

⤙ POISON GIRL OLD FASHIONED ⤚

Poison Girl
Recipe: Brian "Hutch" Wayne
1641 Westheimer Rd #B
Houston, TX 77006
(713) 527-9929

According to an incredibly unscientific poll on my Facebook page, one of the largest selections of whiskey in the state of Texas is at Poison Girl in Houston. It's also one of the great American dive bars. You read that correctly, the best whiskey selection is at a total dive. And it's amazing. Poison Girl is "that bar" in Houston. They just happen to have copious amounts of whiskey. It's had the "greatest dive bar you've ever been to" vibe since the get-go. It's only been recently that Poison Girl has gotten into cocktails, so while not known for their cocktails per say, the Poison Girl Old Fashioned is a fine version to keep in mind next time you want to make one at home.

Glassware: **Old Fashioned Glass**
Garnish: **Orange Peel**

- **2 oz bourbon (Knob Creek)**
- **4 dashes Agnostura orange bitters**
- **1 dash Fee Bros Black Walnut Bitters**
- **1 dash Angostura bitters**
- **.5 oz simple syrup**

1. Add bourbon, bitters, and simple syrup in a mixing glass with ice and stir.

2. Strain into an old fashioned glass, with one large cube of ice.

3. Garnish with an orange peel.

ROSEWATER MIX

- 50% red wine/cardamom syrup
- 25% Rose Combier
- 25% orgeat

To make the red wine syrup, mix white sugar and a moderately robust red wine like malbec in equal proportions at room temperature until dissolved, and add cardamom tincture to taste. We do not heat the syrup. The cardamom tincture is just green cardamom infused in vodka for at least three days.

⤙ ROSEWATER SOUR ⤚

Rosewater
Recipe: Pasha Morshedi
1606 Clear Lake City Blvd
Houston, TX 77062
(832) 224-4182

rosewaterclearlake.com

While working for NASA, Pasha Morshedi spent years collecting and tinkering and finally decided that Clear Lake was ready to enter cocktail culture. Like most of my other favorite bars in Texas, Rosewater is a neighborhood bar. Regulars are learning the differences between styles of vermouth and trying spirits they didn't know existed before Rosewater. That's really, the coolest part of this whole thing. The Rosewater Sour is a quick sipper, so watch yourself. Regarding the recipe, Pasha said, "The Rosewater mix we used to call our secret mix, but we thought that was stupid, so we tell anyone who asks." It's better this way. It's all part of their education.

Glassware: **Coupe Glass**
Garnish: **Rose Tincture**

- • **2 oz floral gin (we use Uncle Val's Restorative, but Hendrick's also works)**
- • **.75 oz lemon juice**
- • **.75 oz Rosewater Mix**
- • **Egg white**

1. Build all ingredients and dry shake.

2. Then shake with ice, and strain into a coupe glass.

3. Decorate the foam with a few drops of a red rose tincture.

—A CONVERSATION WITH—
Bobby Heugel

Tell me about Houston. How did Anvil impact the Houston area?

I actually have a specific opinion about that, but I don't know that it's necessarily as cocktail-y as everybody would like. We built Anvil by ourselves, Kevin and I, with some help from Justin Burrow, who quit the job that he had at the time to come help us build the bar. He just showed up one day and he's like, "I quit and I'm here to help." We're like, "Okay, well, we don't really have any way to pay you."

Justin and I actually drove around Houston and bought all the old bottles of Tanqueray Malacca and sold them on eBay. That's how we paid our bills for the last six months of building Anvil.

We really screwed the opening up of Anvil.

We didn't know what we were doing. We didn't think the cocktails were going to be that popular. It was three of us and Kevin and I had worked together at Beaver's but I basically ran the cocktail program and told Kevin what drinks to make. We didn't train anybody, we just figured it out. Then we just got ran over. It was bad. We were trying to learn how to become business owners and doing all this other stuff, we just didn't know what we were doing.

What was going on in the food scene in Houston at the time that you opened?

There were some good independent restaurants, especially around where Anvil was at, which was why we wanted to put it there. There was DeMarco's, which is probably the best Italian restaurant in Houston. Hugo's was down the street, Mark's, which is closed now, was down the street. It fit really well into a nicer evening, but I don't think that the evening was too fancy. It was still Houstonian in nature.

So the neighborhood embodied the vision for the bar.

Montrose really had an independent spirit that fit us well. Poison Girl, which was our favorite bar, was down the street. We used to go there every single day after we finished working on the bar. It just fit and it made a lot of sense.

~ THE BRAVE ~

Pastry War

This cocktail, The Brave, first appeared on Anvil's menu. In fact, when I asked everyone (who is friends with me in the bar industry on Facebook) what their idea of a quintessential Texas cocktail would be... I had more than one suggestion of The Brave. Bobby Heugel said, "I think it reflects the drinks and style of service at Anvil. We prefer bold drinks built with rustic spirits, made in traditional ways."

Glassware: **Wine Glass**
Garnish: **Orange Zest**

- **1 oz Del Maguey Chichicapa Mezcal**
- **1 oz Tequila Cabeza**
- **.5 oz Averna Amaro**
- **.25 oz Royal Combier Curacao**
- **3 mists of Angostura bitters**

1. Swirl the mezcal, tequila, amaro, and curaçao in a wine glass without ice.

2. Apply three small, evenly distributed mists of Angostura Bitters to the inside of the wine glass above the cocktail.

3. Flame an orange zest on top.

—The Pastry War—

310 MAIN ST
HOUSTON, TX 77002
(713) 225-3310
THEPASTRYWAR.COM

The Pastry War is Texas' first mezcaleria, serving agave spirits from family-owned distilleries. Named after an 1838 conflict between Mexico and France, The Pastry War celebrates the rich and vibrant drinking culture of Mexico with subtle French details throughout the bar. With owner Bobby Heugel's deep passion for promoting sustainability in agave spirits and his involvement with the Tequila Interchange Project, it's no wonder this selection is the best in the state. As the saying goes, Bobby's forgotten more about mezcal than most bartenders will ever learn.

Tongue-Cut Sparrow
310 Main St
Houston, TX 77002
(713) 321-8242

tonguecutsparrow.com

Tongue-Cut Sparrow is a formal cocktail bar inspired by owner Bobby Heugel's travels throughout Japan and Europe. There are 25 seats. There are no signature cocktails. There are hot towels upon arrival. Tongue-Cut Sparrow is a different universe with elite service and a menu that is only classic cocktails. This is the most precise execution you'll see... There is nothing like this anywhere else in Texas.

Glassware: **Cocktail Glass**
Garnish: **Lemon, Olives**

- **2.25 oz Tanqueray No.10 gin**
- **.75 oz 50:50 blend of Dolin Dry and Noilly Prat Original Dry vermouths**

1. Stir with ice and strain into a cocktail glass.

2. Zest lemon and discard.

3. Garnish with two castelvetrano olives.

— Yellow Rose —

So the legend goes, in 1836 at the battle of San Jacinto, a woman by the name of Emily West was, shall we say, "occupying" Santa Anna before the Texan army charged the Mexican camp. The surprise attack ensured General Sam Houston's victory and paved the way for the Republic of Texas. She will always be a Texas legend.

Yellow Rose Distillery is in the process of creating their own legacy through whiskey and education. Yellow Rose launched into the Texas market in 2012 as Houston's first legal whiskey distillery. I was excited and a little apprehensive when I went to visit because I had remembered a Yellow Rose Whiskey I had in the past and, unfortunately, I didn't really like it.

They've grown leaps and bounds. This is great stuff, y'all and others agree. They just won best in class at the American Distilling Institute and a Double at the San Francisco Artisan Spirits. There's always been a bit of a controversy with Yellow Rose (utilizing whiskey from outside of the state to include in blends that are marketed by a distiller named Yellow Rose, with Texas all over the bottle… that whole thing) but honestly, since I last had this to now, they've become good whiskey makers. Maybe it's less sourced product or maybe it's just that they're more experienced now, but regardless, Yellow Rose is solid. They are available across the nation.

— THIRD COAST MULE —

Yellow Rose
Recipe: Houston Farris, Head Distiller/Mixologist
1224 N Post Oak Rd #100
Houston, TX 77055
(281) 886-8757

yellowrosedistilling.com

This simple riff on a Moscow Mule is similar to any Kentucky Mule you'll find, but it's all Texan. It's easy sipping and a great patio drink.

Glassware: **Collins Glass**
Garnish: **Lemon Peel**

- 1.5 oz Yellow Rose blended whiskey
- Ginger beer
- Coconut water
- .75 oz lemon juice
- .75 oz simple syrup

1. Combine ingredients in a shaker with ice and shake vigorously.

2. Strain into a collins glass, filled with ice.

3. Top with equal parts coconut water (no pulp) and Boots (Texas craft soda) Ginger Brew.

4. Garnish with expressed lemon peel.

— FIRE WALK WITH ME —

Stone's Throw
Recipe: Conal Rex Nielsen
1417 Westheimer Rd
Houston, TX 77006
(832) 659-0265

stonesthrowhouston.com

Let's talk orgeat. First, it's pronounced "or-zsa-t" kinda like Zsa Zsa Gabor (it was years before I finally got that one down) and it's a non-alcoholic, almond-based syrup. It's typically seen in tiki drinks, and usually involves orange blossom water or rosewater. Making your own is a bit of a lengthy process as the almonds usually need to soak for about 3–4 hours, but there are some great Texas-based options if you need to procure some quickly. My recommendation is Liber & Son's. It's sweet, nutty, and a great layer to a cocktail. In the Fire Walk with Me from Stone's Throw (a great Montrose area bar in Houston), the nuttiness of the orgeat plays very well with the heat of the jalapenos in this spicy tequila drink.

Glassware: **Coupe Glass**

- 2 oz reposado tequila
- .5 oz falernum
- .5 oz lime juice
- .5 oz orgeat
- 2 slices muddled jalepeno
- Crushed ice

1. Combine ingredients in a shaker with ice and shake vigorously.

2. Strain into coupe glass.

— YOU HAD ME AT HIBISCUS —

Prohibition Supperclub & Bar
1008 Prairie St
Houston, TX 77002
(281) 940-4636
prohibitionhouston.com

If you're going to go there, you might as well commit to it. Prohibition Supper Club is a vaudevillian throw-back that lives in one of the oldest theaters in Houston. From burlesque to Cuban big band music, Prohibition's goal is to give the guests incredible hospitality while simultaneously transporting them back to a different time. The cocktails, however, are delightfully modern, yet nail the simplicity of pre-Prohibition recipes. This might be the most easy-drinking cocktail in the book. And if you're having friends over, make sure you grab that garnish. When it's time to invite the squad over for cocktails, go all the way.

Glassware: **Coupe Glass**
Garnish: **Dehydrated Hibiscus (optional)**

- .5 oz hibiscus syrup
- .75 oz lemon juice
- .25 oz Luxardo
- 1.5 oz reposado tequila

1. Combine ingredients in a shaker with ice and shake vigorously.

2. Double strain into a coupe glass.

3. Garnish with dehydrated hibiscus, if desired.

— WOOSTER'S SOUR —

Recipe: Steven E. Salazar

This is the Wooster's Sour and it's a pretty cool variation on a whiskey sour. So, wait... Why do I often see Angostura or some other bitters on top of cocktails with foam on them? Well, I'm glad you asked! Generally, in this case, the bartender is using the bitters to impact your nose before you even sip the drink at all. The basic idea is that bitters smells better than egg.

Glassware: **Rocks Glass**
Garnish: **Angostura Bitters**

- 1 oz Old Overholt rye whiskey
- 1 oz freshly squeezed and mesh-strained lemon juice
- .75 oz Mathilde Peche cordial
- .5 oz Punch alla Fiamma
- .5 oz turbinado syrup
- 1 egg white

1. Dry shake all ingredients without ice for 10 seconds.

2. Shake with ice for 30 seconds.

3. Fine mesh strain into rocks glass.

4. Top with a dash of Angostura bitters, and use a straw to swirl the ango float into a design.

—Wooster's Garden—

3315 MILAM ST
HOUSTON, TX 77006
(713) 520-0015
WOOSTERSGARDEN.COM

An amazing craft beer selection, paired with an incredibly long menu make for an awesome experience at Wooster's Garden. You can learn a lot about how beverage director Steven Salazar approaches drinks just by perusing the menu. Salazar has an incredible commitment to seasonality that impacts everything in the program.

AUSTIN

★ ★

"TEXAS ISN'T JUST A PLACE ON A MAP...
IT'S AN IDEA IN THE HEARTS OF OUR PEOPLE."

—George P. Bush

When Bill Norris took over the beverage program at Fino in 2005, it was the first introduction of classic craft cocktails to their community in a big way. Bill's perspective on cocktails changed dramatically in 2008 when he traveled to New Zealand for the 42 Below Cocktail World Cup. He, along with other industry legends like Charles Joly, Naren Young, and Ben Carlotto, competed in one of the most bizarre and incredible cocktail competitions I've ever heard of, full of different challenges that wound up changing his perspective on how to approach cocktails. Jump back to Austin, and Bill turns Fino into a machine. He's also now internet buddies with Bobby Heugel, and this whole cocktail thing starts feeling like it could blossom in Texas.

David Alan is another one of those Austin OGs that pushed the envelope in every way possible to further the cocktail scene. He has created training programs for everyone from the home bartender to those who have decided to make this their career, and he is also a powerful voice in the media who championed the new direction booze consumption was moving in Austin. His book, *The Tipsy Texan,* was the literary introduction to the Texas cocktail scene. With Bill and David at the helm, the shift in Austin's bar scene towards cocktails was inevitable.

Austin is a relentlessly casual town. More often than not, fanciness is condemned, and this creates a fantastically approachable food and beverage scene. Austin cocktail bars focus on making great tasting, fresh, and approachable drinks for folks in anything from cowboy boots to flip flops. Some very determined people spent a lot of effort to turn Austin into a force on the national cocktail scene.

★ ★

⚊ LOVEJOY ⚊

There are no cocktails at Nickel City, at least, not by that name. The word has been intentionally left off of all menus and the drinks are all under $10. The Lovejoy is a deliciously balanced blend of Mexican ingredients. For the shrub, follow the simple shrub recipe from D&D Shrubs and Syrups.

Glassware: **Can**
Garnish: **Grapefruit Half Moon**

- **1 oz Altos Tequila**
- **.75 oz El Silencio Mezcal**
- **.75 oz fresh lime juice**
- **.75 oz watermelon prickly pear shrub**
- **6 drops of sea salt water**

1. Combine ingredients in a shaker with ice and shake vigorously.

2. Strain over pebble ice and garnish.

—Nickel City—

1133 E 11TH ST
AUSTIN, TX 78702
NICKELCITYBAR.COM

There are two areas at Nickel City… the main area, and then the pop-up bar in the back. They call it Cash Only, because, well, it is. It's already hosted some of the country's best bartenders, pop-up-style, all for charitable causes. "It's different when you're opening a place where you plan on it being forever," said beverage director, Travis Tober. And Nickel City, while certainly nicer and much more likely to make you a decent Sazerac, elicits the same feelings as Longbranch Inn, which used to be where Nickel City is now, did… and they were opened for almost a century. Regarding the name, Travis said, "It's actually named after a rough neighborhood in Buffalo that was home to a lot of Polish immigrants. Always liked the contrast of the name."

— SOTOL RECALL —

Backbeat
Recipe: Steph Teslar
1300 S Lamar Blvd
Austin, TX 78704
(512) 551-9980
backbeat-atx.com

Although it began as a pop-up during the La Dolce Vita Food & Wine Festival, Backbeat is now another great neighborhood cocktail bar serving those imbibing in South Austin. There's a little prep that comes with this cocktail, but, trust me, once you have made the Backbeat Blueberry Bounce, you'll find all sorts of ways to use it at home (Try it on vanilla ice cream.) I also love the use of Zucca, which has flavors of rhubarb and Chinese herbs, making it pleasant, yet bitter. Side note: every time I hear the name of this bar, I want to finish an Oasis lyric. Every. Time.

Glassware: **Collins Glass**
Garnish: **Blueberries**

- • **1.5 oz sotol**
- • **.5 oz Zucca Amaro**
- • **.75 oz Blueberry Bounce**
- • **.75 oz fresh lemon juice**
- • **Egg white**
- • **2 dashes lavender bitters**

1. Combine all ingredients and dry shake without ice for 10 seconds.

2. Shake with ice for 30 seconds.

3. Fine mesh strain into a collins glass.

4. Top with soda and garnish with blueberries.

Blueberry Bounce

Place 6 cups of blueberries in a saucepan. Lightly smash berries open with a muddler or spoon. Add 1 bottle of Texas red wine blend and 1 cup of sugar. Simmer on low for 10 minutes or until berries start losing color/looking cooked. Remove from heat and add 2 tablespoons of Texas Wild Herb Blend— Sage, rosemary, lavender, and thyme. Stir to incorporate. Allow to cool and then fine strain.

In this particular cocktail, the base spirit is sotol. Let me make one thing clear... sotol is not agave. "Sotol is a spirit elaborated in Northern Mexico from the Dasylirion plant. A relative of the agave plant, Sotol has its own denomination of origin and can be produced in the States of Chihuahua, Coahuila, and Durango. Typically it is produced in the same artisanal fashion as mezcal," says Ricardo Pico, founder of Sotol Clande. In addition to Mexico, sotol also has an interesting history in Texas, and I wouldn't be surprised to see a Texas-produced sotol in the next few years, if not months. Until then, feel free to try Sotol Clande. It's delicious.

⇥ THROWING SHADE ⇤

Recipe: Jessica Sanders

This particular drink, Throwing Shade, is a beautiful way to see how Japanese whisky can be accented and not merely over-powered. Owner Jessica Sanders said, "I enjoy drinking Japanese whisky but am also hesitant to use it in cocktails (especially those with citrus) for fear of covering up all the delicate flavors. This sour is spicy and bright and fits in the 'just rich enough without going overboard' family so as to allow the whisky to shine through."

Glassware: **Coupe Glass**

- 1.5 oz Japanese whisky (such as Suntory TOKI)
- .75 oz fresh grapefruit juice (Texas ruby red grapefruit is ideal)
- .5 oz Zucca Amaro
- .5 oz ginger syrup (Austin-based Liber & Co. brand)
- 1 dash Peychaud's bitters

1. Combine ingredients in a shaker with ice and shake vigorously.

2. Fine strain into a chilled cocktail coupe.

—drink. well.—

207 E 53RD ST
AUSTIN, TX 78751
(512) 614-6683
DRINKWELLAUSTIN.COM

Jessica Sanders is, unquestionably, the godmother of the Austin cocktail scene, and her program at drink.well. has produced some of Austin's best craft cocktail minds. From drink.well. being named Food & Wine magazine's "Top 100 New Bars in America" to Jessica herself landing in the finals of both Speed Rack and the Bacardi Legacy competitions, the reputation is impeccable.

— Tito's —

Tito started it all. He opened the first legal distillery in Texas.
He basically worked with the Texas Alcoholic Beverage
Commission to craft the laws that would govern future distillers.
He, essentially, started the Texas spirits revolution. We owe a
lot to Tito.

As Tito likes to say, "everyone thought he was crazy," and
that's pretty evident considering that there wasn't even
another distiller's permit issued until almost 10 years after Tito.
There are currently 108 active distiller licenses in Texas, and 87
of them were issued after Tito had been in business for 15
years. Let that sink in. What was distilling in America before
Tito? It was a glimmer.

Tito's is simply Tito's. They have no line extensions. They are
not barrel aging anything or secretly working on a gin. They
make the vodka that got people to start calling their name in
bars across the United States. I've probably consumed more
Tito's in New York than I ever have in Texas.

Tito's is simply the success story that all Texas spirits are
emulating in some capacity. Tito is the king and for that, craft
distillers, specifically in Texas, will always be grateful for the
path that he's paved. Guess he wasn't crazy after all.

Tito's

titosvodka.com

One of the drinks that Texans cut their teeth on is certainly the Texas Tea (or whatever you want to call vodka with sweet tea). This tastes like your sophomore year.

Glassware: **Highball Glass**

Garnish: **Mint Sprig**

- ◦ **1.5 oz Tito's Handmade Vodka**
- ◦ **1.5 oz freshly brewed tea**
- ◦ **.75 oz orange curacao liqueur**
- ◦ **.75 oz fresh sour mix**
- ◦ **Dash of honey**

1. Combine all ingredients in highball glass with ice.

2. Stir well to combine.

3. Garnish and serve.

TEXAS GRAPEFRUIT

If Texas grapefruits are in season, by all means amplify the measure of grapefruit juice in the cocktail.

— THE HATCHBACK —

Firehouse Lounge
Recipe: Paul Neuenschwander, Asst Manager/
Lead Bartender, Firehouse Lounge, Austin, TX

Craft dive. The idea behind Firehouse Lounge was to create a "craft dive" bar. The building itself was Austin's oldest fire station, built in 1885, and Firehouse Lounge is on the first floor of what is now the Firehouse Hostel. That, in and of itself can come in handy if you happen to go a little too hard. In case you haven't figured it out by now, you're going to find a lot of grapefruit in Texas cocktails. What can I say? We have the best grapefruit on the planet, and frankly, it goes pretty well with agave spirits. Regarding the Hatchback, Firehouse's lead bartender Paul Neuenschwander said, "The drink is definitely reminiscent of a Siesta Cocktail, but appropriately lengthened with our beloved Topo Chico and subtly sweetened for the Texas summer, which is half the year in Austin."

Glassware: **Mason Jar**
Garnish: **Orange Twist**

- **1.5 oz blanco tequila**
- **.75 oz Campari**
- **.5 oz fresh lime juice**
- **.5 oz fresh Texas ruby red grapefruit juice**
- **.5 oz simple syrup**
- **Topo Chico**
- **Orange twist**

1. Shake and strain all ingredients into and ice-filled mason jar.

2. Top with Topo Chico, and add a healthy twist of orange and a straw.

—A CONVERSATION WITH —
Chris Bostick

So, tell me about you man, where are you from?

Born in Corpus Christi, there for six months. All my family grew
up, you know, kind of Central Austin. Went to elementary school in
Austin. Went to high school in Leander. I was in Austin until '96 when
I moved to NYC and I was there until 2001, when I returned to Austin.

Fast forward to 2002 and I started working at Fonda San Miguel. I
had worked with Miguel, in New York, and he was back in Austin at
that point, so he was like, "yeah, I'll get you the job here." And so,
that was a place that I was given this opportunity to take the reins
and run the bar program. I had a budget and wrote the cocktail
menus and tried to elevate what they were doing.

Then, in the middle of 2007, I moved to LA, kind of chased a gal
out there. I worked at the Beverly Hills Hotel doing cocktails at the
pool bar, and then also working at 1912, which is like the deluxe hotel
lobby bar. But then from there, I severely fractured my collar bone
snowboarding in Southern California, and I was out of commission for
months, so I started a blog. If I was going to be out of work for six to
eight months, I wanted to find a way to stay involved and keep this
momentum going.

So what happened?

Well, ultimately I got hired at the Varnish, and that was like everything I had learned up to this point in my career had led me to that
moment. That's when I realized very quickly that if I stick with this, it
could be the key to opening up my own bar in Austin. And enough, a
handful of years down the road, we did it. Half Step was born.

Worth the wait?

Half Step has been the hardest job I've ever done in my life, and continues to be one of the hardest things ever, but the magic happens outside of your comfort zone. So, there's been no denying that Half Step's put me out of my comfort zone on many occasion. That's where you learn.

So, we opened February of 2014.

What was the cocktail scene in Austin like at that point?

It was budding. There certainly wasn't anybody doing our style, you know, there were still a lot of ingredients in cocktails, still a lot of unbridled creativity, which isn't necessarily a bad thing, but I don't think that the hospitality was really dialed in at that point. Half Step was really more vocal about simple, great drinks with amazing service. Simplicity doesn't mean low quality.

What do you mean, specifically?

Simplicity, if anything else, I think is more difficult than ... some people just keep adding on more ingredients until they think it's okay. A little bit of knowledge is dangerous for a young cocktail community. Because all of the sudden, people think that they're experts, and they're armed with this headstrong hubris. We're getting out of that. For a long time, it seemed that Austin was very full of itself, and now we're kind of coming back to Earth and realizing that "hey, good cocktail bars doesn't mean that we have to do everything so complex."

~ GINGER PALOMA ~

Half Step
Recipe: Chris Bostick, Owner, Half Step
75 1/2 Rainey St
Austin, TX 78701
(512) 391-1877

halfstepbar.com

When Texas' own Chris Bostick found himself in LA running one of the hottest cocktail bars in the world, The Varnish, he knew it was a stepping stone. (Or a half stepping stone! Get it?) He knew he wanted to come back to Austin and open up his own place, and he knew he had the team to do so. Half Step entered the Rainey Street scene in Austin when it was only speed bars. They saw it as an opportunity to create an unexpected experience for their guest. It's also a bartender factory with some of the best bartenders in Texas coming through the program. This has been ranked among the best bars in the world, and it's incredibly easy to see why.

Glassware: **Collins Glass**
Garnish: **Grapefruit Wedge**

- 2 oz Tequila Ocho
- 1 fresh ruby red grapefruit
- .5 oz fresh lime juice
- .25 oz ginger syrup
- 2.5 oz seltzer water

1. Shake all ingredients except for the seltzer with 2 tablespoons crushed ice.

2. Pour into a frozen, ice filled collins glass, top with seltzer, and garnish with a grapefruit wedge and a pinch of kosher salt.

— Still Austin —

440 E ST ELMO RD
AUSTIN, TX 78745
(512) 276-2700
STILLAUSTIN.COM

Still Austin is brand new, but their programs are interesting enough that I wanted to make sure to include them in our list of great Texas spirits. Initially conceived in 2013 by three families, Still is the first whiskey distillery in Austin's city limits since Prohibition. Helmed by head distiller John Schrepel, Still mills, mashes, ferments, distills, barrels, and bottles all of their products in-house. They utilize local grains, limestone-filtered water, and the Texas climate to make their whiskeys.

Still founded a project called the 1919 Heritage Grains project. This is a multi-year effort to reintroduce antique grains that were grown in abundance prior to Prohibition, but have all but disappeared. In 1919, the USDA did its first national grain survey, so we have a very good idea of what wheat was growing in Texas in 1919 and in what quantities. It ends up that most of the wheat growing in Texas back then was soft red winter wheat.

Soft winter wheat also happens to be the right wheat for making whiskey. Lisa Braunberg, one of Still's co-founders, told me, "1919 is of interest to us because the 18th Amendment passed that year, so we like to think of it as the last good year for the American spirits industry. We want to do is go back to 1919 Texas and re-introduce some of the most popular Wheat varieties of the time."

They also offer several unique programs including a DYOB (Distill Your Own Barrel) program, where groups can learn the craft of distilling from beginning to end of the process. Still currently sells new make whiskeys, including New Make (corn, wheat, barley), Mother Pepper Whiskey (Chile Pequin peppers, Smoked Serrano peppers, and aji amarillo peppers), and Daydreamer Whiskey (Valencia Oranges, Tangelo, and Beramont Citrus) that are currently only available at the distillery in Austin, but by the time this book comes out, they'll probably have distribution.

— BOLIVIAN BIBLE THUMPER —

Holy Roller
Recipe: Jennifer Keyser—Holy Roller
509 Rio Grande St
Austin, TX 78701
(512) 502-5119

holyrolleraustin.com

Timing is everything. If I had finished working on this book any sooner, I would have missed the opportunity to see the incredible program Jen Keyser has built at Holy Roller. This female-lead-punk-rock-brunch-all-day hot spot is one of the coolest experiences in Austin. This cocktail highlights Singani, a pomace brandy distilled from white Muscat of Alexandria grapes. This Bolivian spirit has been around since the 1600s, but is just starting to make its way onto back bars in the United States Jen said. "I wanted something fun with a bit of religious kitsch. Being that we're called Holy Roller, I thought it would make for a unique and brand—appropriate cocktail name." Reverence, frankly, be damned.

Glassware: Coupe Glass

- 1.5 oz Rujero Singani
- .25 oz Chareau Aloe Liqueur
- .25 oz Demerara syrup
- .75 oz grapefruit juice
- 1 egg white

1. Dry shake without ice for 10 seconds.

2. Shake with ice for 30 seconds.

3. Fine mesh strain into a coupe glass.

4. Add one dash of Angostura on top.

— Revolution Spirits —

When co-founders Aaron Day and Mark Shilling decided to push forward with an idea hatched six years earlier, they did so because they saw the pending revolution. Coming from a government relations and public policy background, they were just as intrigued with helping build the Texas craft spirits industry as they were with creating spirits. "We got a lot of mentorship with some of the best craft distillers in the nation by swapping our government relations knowledge," said Aaron.

Revolution assembled a team of brewers turned distillers who agreed with their vision for testing the boundaries of spirits production and collaboration. Revolution is a seemingly endless revolving door of experimentation. They make a coffee liqueur with a favorite Austin coffee roaster, Cuvee coffee. They make fruit liqueurs from spent fruit from the famed Jester King Brewery. They offer apple brandy from Argus's hard cider. They swap barrels with brewers, vineyards, whiskey, and mezcal distilleries for their Single Barrel aged gin series.

"Economically, you need to start with an unaged spirit, so we made a gin that we could experiment with that was to be our flagship product," said Aaron. Austin Reserve Gin is a well-balanced gin with botanicals inspired by the terroir of Central Texas. With hints of rosemary, juniper, and lavender, the gin is presented at a 100 proof, which heightens the finish of the remaining ingredients of lemon grass, pink peppercorn, and hand-zested grapefruit.

Their latest release is a fantastic companion to their flagship gin product, as it is the first Texas amaro.

"My great-grandfather ran moonshine as a kid on his bicycle in the hills of Tennessee and I think Mark has a family connection to a rye whiskey that didn't make it past Prohibition," Aaron told me. I'm glad they've "gone legit" and decided to help grow this industry in Texas. Not only are they some of the most creative spirit makers in Texas, but they're on the forefront of legislative changes that will make it easier for all of us to enjoy this burgeoning industry.

~ TEXAS NEGRONI ~

Revolution Spirits
12345 Pauls Valley Rd
Austin, TX 78737
(512) 358-1203

revolutionspirits.com

This is as Texas as it gets, y'all. 100% Texas ingredients in this classic Negroni recipe.

Glassware: **Rocks Glass**
Garnish: **Grapefruit**

- **2 oz Austin Reserve Gin**
- **1 oz Amico Amaro**
- **1 oz rouge vermouth**
- **Grapefruit peel**

1. Place a large ice cube in a rocks glass.

2. Combine gin, amaro, and vermouth in the glass and stir to combine.

3. Rub the rim of the glass with grapefruit peel garnish.

4. Finish with a small Austin Reserve Gin float.

~ QUARTZ COMPOSER ~

Juniper
Recipe: Justin Elliott
2400 E Cesar Chavez St #304
Austin, TX 78702
(512) 220-9421
juniperaustin.com

Located in East Austin, Juniper is a mix of the rich flavors of Texas and culinary traditions of Northern Italy. Since opening in 2015, the neighborhood restaurant has gained attention and support as a rising star in the local community, boasting accolades like "Best New Restaurants" in *Austin Monthly*, and "Top 25 Restaurants," by the *Austin American-Statesmen*. It makes sense as Justin Elliot run programs are known as some of the top cocktail programs in the city. I asked him about the orgin of the name and he told me a story about a Macbook glitching and flashing the words "quartz composer" on the screen. He said, "But one reason I thought it sounded 'right,' is the 'quartz' kind of speaks to the minerality of mezcal, but also the almost shimmery top notes of the anise from both the Sambuca and the Mexican mint garnish."

Glassware: **Old Fashioned Glass**
Garnish: **Mexican Mint Marigold**

- .75 oz Old Highborn Gin
- .75 oz Mezcal Vago
- .75 oz canary melon syrup
- .25 oz sambuca
- .5 oz lime juice

1. Shake all ingredients and strain into an old fashioned glass over ice.

2. Top with Peychaud's and a Mexican mint marigold.

— Emerald Absinthe —

Texas absinthe is a very real thing. But before we get into that, let's get a few things straight. First, absinthe does not cause hallucinations. You are no more likely to see a giant Pokémon eating your Doritos after drinking absinthe than if you were drinking vodka or tequila. Second, the absinthe in the US is "real" absinthe. The majority of United States brands are made with grand wormwood, and they are usually better than a lot of their European counterparts.

Lastly, absinthe drips are real lighting your absinthe on fire is marketing. This little "tradition" showed up in the 90s (The 1990s, to clarify). Those who resort to this marketing and sensationalism are usually just using vodka with some anise and green food coloring.

Emerald Absinthe is a wine-based spirit steeped with 13 herbs and spices including anise, fennel, and grand wormwood, creating a creamy, lingering finish with notes of licorice and green pepper, and a hint of golden raisins.

After distillation the absinthe then endures a second 10-day maceration of herbs, allowing the liquid to change colors with the natural green color of the chlorophyll. Master Distiller Matt Mancuso developed his blend of select botanicals from traditional, early 19th Century French and Swiss absinthe styles. "It's actually closer to what was made in the 1790s than anything in the past 100 years," said co-founder Jessica Graves.

— GREEN GODDESS PUNCH —

Emerald Absinthe
Recipe: Jessica Leigh Graves
704 Hwy 71
Bastrop, TX 78602
(512) 766-5090

derelictairship.com

The recipe is for a punch but don't be afraid to just toss Emerald Absinthe in some champagne or prosecco. This punch is light but full of beautiful notes of anise.

Glassware: **Collins Glass**
Garnish: **Mint, Lime, or Cucumber**

- .5 oz Emerald absinthe
- 1 oz lime juice
- 1 oz simple syrup
- 4 oz Topo Chico

1. Add absinthe, simple syrup, and lime to a collins glass and stir.

2. Top with Topo Chico.

3. Garnish with mint, lime, or cucumber.

— *Genius Gin* —

The folks at Genius Gin love gin. They've focused their entire journey around their love of gin... as they say, gin is the only vodka worth drinking. Mike Groener, founder of Genius told me, "Upon researching gin and learning about its fall from fame to the hands of the more neutral alternative, vodka, we quickly realized that not only was gin a large cultural part of history, but it was often misunderstood. A whole world of gins exist; in all flavors and colors."

Genius's Old Highborn Gin, is making quite the impression in Texas. It's a traditional dry spirit with a Texas flair, and, unlike most gins, it's pot distilled to retain deep flavors and oils. It's incredibly fresh with hints of cinnamon, tea, citrus peels, and juniper.

Aaron Kimmel, formely of drink.well., began this cocktail as a play on a classic Corpse Reviver. He also uses Cocchi Americano Rosa, which is slightly more bitter and aromatic than the classic Cocchi. It's almost a light Aperol and is incredibly delicious.

Genius Gin
4202 Santiago St #2
Austin, TX 78745
(512) 710-7907

geniusliquids.com

Aclassic drink for a classic gin. This is one recipe you should commit to memory and bust out the next time someone tells you they "hate" gin.

Glassware: **Coupe Glass**
Garnish: **Grapefruit Peel**

- 1.5 oz Genius Original
- .75 oz Cocchi Americano Rosa
- .75 oz fresh grapefruit juice
- .25 oz fresh lemon juice
- .75 oz Gran Classico
- Absinthe spray (Tenneyson preferred)

1. Pour the gin, cocchi, juices, and Gran Classico into a cocktail shaker with ice and shake.

2. Spray glass with absinthe, or rinse.

3. Strain into a glass.

4. Garnish with grapefruit peel.

⤙ HOT MESS ⤚

VOX Table
Recipe: Madelyn Kay
1100 S Lamar Blvd #2140
Austin, TX 78704
(512) 375-4869

voxtableaustin.business.site

Lead by beverage director Madelyn Kay, the VOX Table has been one of the most innovative programs in Austin since its inception. While other cocktail programs have a tendency to haphazardly assemble brunch cocktails, it's a point of emphasis at VOX. This is a spicy, agave-filled cocktail and this thing's delicious, y'all.

Glassware: **Rocks Glass**
Garnish: **Lemon Wheel**

- **1.75 oz reposado tequila (Altos)**
- **.75 oz fresh lemon juice**
- **.5 oz serrano grenadine**
- **.33 oz Cholula hot sauce**

1. Combine ingredients in a shaker with ice and shake vigorously.

2. Strain into a rocks glass.

3. Garnish with lemon wheel.

~ TARRAGUEUR ~

Roosevelt Room
Recipe: Justin Lavenue
307 W 5th St
Austin, TX 78701
(512) 494-4094

therooseveltroomatx.com

Austin's Justin Lavenue is one of the world's best bartenders...
Want proof? He won Bombay Sapphire's Most Imaginative
Bartender a couple years back. That's reason enough to go to Roosevelt Room. The massive cocktail menu is broken into various eras
and the cocktails invented during each. Now, obviously, you could
just defer to the Roosevelt Room signature cocktails... I hear there's a
pretty decent bartender there. The Tarragueur is a Texas twist on the
classic De Rigueer. That cocktail first appeared in 1927 in *Here's How*
by Norman Hume Anthony, otherwise known as Judge Junior.

Glassware: **Nick & Nora**
Garnish: **Tarragon Sprig, Grapefruit Peel**

- **1.5 oz Texas whiskey of your choosing (We like it with Balcones Single Malt and/or Balcones True Blue Cask Strength)**
- **1 oz Texas ruby red grapefruit juice**
- **.5 oz honey syrup (1:1)**
- **1 small (around 1" x 1") grapefruit peel**
- **8–10 Texas tarragon leaves**
- **1 dash saline tincture (1:10)**

1. Shake all ingredients well over one large ice cube.

2. Single-strain into a Nick & Nora glass.

3. Garnish with three sprays of ten-year Islay Scotch, one tarragon
sprig, and a grapefruit peel.

— Fat Ice —

1340 AIRPORT COMMERCE DR SUITE 200
AUSTIN, TEXAS 78741
(512) 351-6767
FATICE.COM

Javier Flores is relentless. He knew what his vision was for the company he wanted to start and he didn't give up until he achieved it. He's also one of the most laid back, cool dudes you'll ever meet. Everyone loves Javi. He's the craft ice man.

I know what you're thinking... craft ice? Absolutely. Ice is one of the most important elements of your drink. Unless you're making The Brave, water is in every single cocktail. If I order a Balcones Brimstone and it shows up in a glass, full of sonic ice, looking like a watered down coke... I'm not happy. Neither are you. They need the Ice Man with that Fat Ice. I chatted with Javi about his journey.

What were you doing before you started Fat Ice?

I have been in the service industry for the better part of two decades and I guess you can say I slowly evolved to this. The majority of my time I was behind the bar, but I managed restaurants, waited tables, and was even a DJ for a bit. I worked across the state in all sorts of venues, but my favorite was working in restaurants. They fascinate me and are where I feel I found my focus. Moving to Austin I had three failed attempts at opening a business that had ice involved in some way or another, but never quite got it right. Some people say the third time is the charm, but for me I guess it was the fourth.

I'm assuming you saw an opportunity, but did you have a particular interest in ice before starting your company?

I was an arrogant bartender for a while and always told myself that no one was going to do something better than me. Ice was no exception to that. I traditionally take my drinks neat and drink my sodas and beverages at room temperature when available. So as far as personal

consumption, I never really used ice up until recently. When I did first see hand-cut ice was on a R&D trip I took in 2011, and knew immediately that it was something special and really made a difference in drinks and cocktails. I brought it into a restaurant in South Texas that I was running at the time and slowly went from 30 to 40 cocktails in a night to over 250 in a night all served on hand-cut ice.

I loved my hometown, but knew the only way to further my career was to move to a major market and try to stir and shake with the best of them. I moved to Austin and I saw that only one bar had a clinebell machine at the time and that was Weather Up. With many more cocktail bars set to open and none with access to clinebell ice, I saw an opportunity and decided to seize it.

Why is ice important to cocktails?

Ice is important because it really is the foundation to most all modern cocktails. Whether it is used to chill, dilute, or for presentation, ice is involved in the majority of cocktails today. The most common forgotten ingredient in cocktails is water, which is usually incorporated using ice. I like to say that ice is the equivalent to the flame a chef uses to cook; it is the foundation that everything else is built on. I can say without a doubt, cocktails as we know them today would not exist without ice.

What makes Fat Ice special?

This is something that I have to keep asking myself every day and is what pushes me to constantly want to do better and bigger. I feel that over the past year that Fat Ice has been in business it has changed not only the local ice game, but has made an impact nationally as well. High-quality clinebell ice used to be something hard to come by, but thanks to the Fat Ice business model it is more accessible than ever before. Fat Ice currently affects more drinks than any other craft ice or large format ice business in the country. We currently have distribution throughout Texas and have had our ice used at festivals and special events across the country. The pride my staff and I take in the product I feel really shows.

What is your process?

I only cut my ice in a freezer, which sets me apart from most other people. Most people choose to cut ice wet in a tempered environment, but I find this yields inconsistent cubes that vary in size. Fat Ice is cut frozen, packed frozen, and shipped in marine-grade coolers to make sure that the product arrives in pristine condition.

How has the reception been to Fat Ice?

The reception has been better than I could have expected. I knew my friends and colleagues would like it, but I always wondered about the general consumer. I went from being "Javi" to "The Ice Man" in a matter of months. People are excited about the product's accessibility and ease of use, as compared to harvesting and doing the work yourself, which is the other way to get clear ice in your bars. It is really nice to have earned the respect of your peers for something that you have put so much into.

What's the weirdest/coolest ice project you've taken on?

This past year I was asked if I could make a special cut for a certain "Big Game" in Houston, Texas. This is the moment when I knew this product had potential that I had not even imagined yet. Along with being at major sporting events and festivals/concerts, I take a lot of pride in knowing that the best chefs and bartenders from all over the world use my product in their programs. Getting asked by a guy you just saw on *Chef's Table* on Netflix if you could cut specialty ice for his event I would say ranks up there.

— Small — Victory

108 E 7TH ST
AUSTIN, TX 78701
(737) 701-0500
SMALLVICTORY.BAR

Small Victory is weird, y'all. It's in a weird building with a weird door that takes up some weird spiral staircase... but then you open the door. It's shocking how opposite it feels inside. It's cozy and comfortable, cool but not pretentious, fashionable but not obnoxious and that's before you even have a chance to look at the menu. Owner and beverage director Josh Loving has an incredible background including beverage director at Jeffrey's and Josephine House, opening Weather Up, and running Half Step's ice program. And why not? He started at Fino (where the cocktails in Austin began) with Bill Norris.

⇀ CAMPARI COLADA ⇀

Small Victory feels like a symphony. There are angles and layers that are the work of a perfectionist designing to their exact mies en plas... and it's incredible. This, truly, was one of my favorite cocktails in this book. You've chosen wisely. Make this one.

Glassware: **Tiki Glass**
Garnish: **Orange Slice, Brandied Cherry**

- **3 oz fresh pineapple juice**
- **1 oz coconut cream**
- **1 oz heavy whipping cream**
- **2 oz Campari**

1. Whip-shake without ice and pour over crushed ice in a tall tiki glass that holds 15 ounces or more, and swizzle.

2. Garnish with an orange slice and a brandied cherry.

— SoCo Ginger Beer —

One of the new kids on the block is SoCo Ginger Beer. Beginning in the mid 18th century, traditional ginger beer was alcoholic and made using ginger root, lemons, and sugar to create a light and refreshing beer. SoCo uses those same great ingredients to brew a non-alcoholic version, while keeping true to traditionally strong ginger and citrus flavors. Then they take that and offer a variety of seasonal flavors.

SoCo Ginger Beer is rooted in Austin but also produced in Denton, by brothers David and Benjamin Weaver. Together, they do five farmer's markets as well as wholesaling to local bars and restaurants. David told me, "We were tired of drinking carbonated water pretending to be ginger beer. It took us more than a year, but we've made the real thing from only fresh fruit, fresh vegetables, and organic sugar cane that tastes better than we could have hoped. No chemicals disguised as 'natural flavors'. No preservatives. No high fructose anything. Just clean, crisp beer made with the freshest ingredients we could find."

My toddler highly recommends the Hibiscus version, while I found myself loving the Jalapeno-Lime. That, my friends, is a very easy way to kick your mules up a notch. In fact, here's your recipe to do so.

— MEXICAN MULE —

SoCo Ginger Beer
4550 Mueller Blvd
Austin, TX 78704
(512) 387-1955
socogingerbeer.com

A simple mule with a bit of a kick. The spice of the ginger beer pairs perfectly with tequila, instead of vodka, in this twist on a Moscow Mule.

Glassware: **Mason Jar**
Garnish: **Grapefruit Slice**

- **4 oz Jalapeño Lime SoCo Ginger Beer**
- **2 oz tequila**
- **2 oz squeezed grapefruit**
- **.5 oz agave syrup**

1. Assemble all ingredients in a mason jar and gently stir.

2. Garnish with a grapefruit slice.

GOMA FASHION

Water Trade
Recipe: Whitney Hazelmyer
1603 South Congress Avenue
Austin, TX 78704
(512) 920-6405

"**T**here has always been a special place in my heart for savory flavors in cocktails as they presented a delicious challenge. Recently, my coworker was experimenting with a toasted sesame tincture, and it made its way into a coconut and rum cocktail of mine, but the texture of the oil needed something more simple to shine through. I decided to fat wash a rye whisky with the toasted sesame oil and throw in a little vanilla, and that was all it needed. I diluted and pre-batched it for consistency, accuracy, and to keep at a frosty temp, because I like my old fashioneds cold. A cook in the Otoko kitchen and I teamed up to make some Angostura candy that you could stir in, but it is best to reserve that for less humid climates."—Whitney Hazelmyer, bartender

Glassware: **Rocks Glass**
Garnish: **Luxurado Cherry**

- **2 oz toasted sesame oil washed rye whisky**
- **.5 oz Giffard Madagascar vanille**
- **.25 oz turbinado simple syrup**
- **3 dashes Angostura and orange bitters**

1. Pour ingredients over ice and stir for 20 seconds.

2. Top with a Luxardo cherry.

— Treaty Oak —

507 BAYLOR ST
AUSTIN, TX 78703
(512) 974-6700
TREATYOAKDISTILLING.COM

When Treaty Oak started, the only spirits being made in Texas were vodkas. "There was some white paper forecasting saying that rum was going to grow rapidly as a category and possibly be the next craze. I don't know if Bacardi paid people to write that, but that obviously didn't happen," laughed Nate Powell, partner at Treaty Oak. Knowing they didn't want to start with vodka and needing something unaged to begin with, they started to make the first Texas rum.

Treaty Oak Platinum Rum was also the first Texas spirit entirely sourced from Texas. They use molasses from the last sugar mill in Texas. "The molasses was actually a byproduct in the process of making sugar and it was an expense. We started buying it and made it a profit center for them, which helped keep them going. It's a really cool story," said Nate. He also told me that he knew of a few other rums that were using the same sugar mill to source their molasses as well.

The first version of the Treaty Oak distillery included a 10 gallon, homemade still, built by Founder Daniel Barnes' father in law, located in a business park in North Austin. They'd take the molasses beer and dump it into the seven-inch opening of the still. Nate told me, "If you can imagine, this wasn't a perfect process. Usually you'd get most of it in there, but towards the end you'd get a little impatient, you'd get some spills going on. Then we were pouring into mason jars... that's how little we got out of it. People want to say small batch or craft and I just don't know if it gets more defined by our process that we went through."

Now, visiting Treaty Oak is one of the coolest experiences you can have in Texas. No, it's not still in a business park. Treaty Oak Ranch is 28 acres and is now one of the anchors on the famous Fitzhugh Road outside of Dripping Springs. Treaty Oak has always been an innovator and they are currently moving into a very experimental version of its former self. From utilizing smoked poblano peppers (infusion is too strong of a word), to a Dripping Spring only botanical gin, to rye versions of all their whiskies, their laboratory series is some of the most innovative distilling happening in Texas.

~ HILL COUNTRY HIGHBALL ~

The Highball is making a comeback and bartenders are recognizing the skill it takes to serve a great Highball. The Highball first appeared in 1900 in Harry Johnson's *Bartenders Manual*. Highballs have a larger proportion of a non-alcoholic mixer than their base spirit. When made well, they are simple, delicate, and incredibly refreshing.

Glassware: **Highball Glass**
Garnish: **Rosemary Sprig, Grapefruit Zest**

- **2 oz Treaty Oak whiskey**
- **Waterloo Sparkling Water**
- **.75 oz rosemary simple syrup**

1. Stir whiskey and simple syrup in a highball glass with ice.

2. Top with Waterloo Sparkling Water.

3. Garnish with a sprig of rosemary and a grapefruit zest.

Rosemary Simple Syrup

- **1 cup sugar**
- **1 cup water**
- **2–3 sprigs of rosemary**

1. Simmer mixture for 10–15 minutes.

2. Strain and store in the refrigerator.

This cocktail is from Aisling Gammill, who has been at Whisler's for over three years. Maggie Bailey was one of Prohibition's most notorious bootleggers and, in this cocktail, the use of white whiskey (otherwise known as moonshine) is another throwback. If you're looking for a good white whiskey for this, check out Still Austin. Go ahead, make it super local.

Glassware: Rocks Glass
Garnish: Thyme Sprig

- **2 oz white whiskey**
- **.5 oz Dolin Dry**
- **.75 oz heavy whipping cream**
- **.75 oz roasted corn syrup**

1. Combine ingredients in a shaker with ice and shake vigorously.

2. Pour over ice in a rocks glass, and garnish with thyme sprig.

Roasted Corn Syrup

- **2 cups corn kernels**
- **1 cup fresh thyme**
- **1 tsp salt**
- **1 tsp ground black pepper**
- **1 tsp vegetable oil**
- **1–2 cups sugar**
- **3 cups water**

Preheat oven to 400°F. On a baking sheet toss together corn, oil, salt, and pepper. Spread evenly on sheet and bake for 12–15 minutes, turning a couple of times until the kernels start to turn golden-brown. Remove corn from oven and transfer to a saucepot along with water and thyme. Simmer uncovered for about 15–20 minutes until the corn has released all of its starch and the stock starts to take on a slightly milky appearance. Strain off and reserve the liquid. Measure the amount of stock and add an equal amount of sugar. Stir to dissolve.

—Whisler's—

1816 E 6TH ST
AUSTIN, TX 78702
(512) 480-0781
WHISLERSATX.COM

Whisler's just feels cool, like there are secrets here... or maybe that's just the mezcaleria on the second floor. Mezcalería Tobalá is one of the first bars in Texas to focus on mezcal. Stepping into Tobalá makes you feel like you've been transported to Oaxaca. It's a place for conversation and education through some of the most beautiful spirits in the world.

In a building constructed in 1917, Whisler's was built to bridge the gap between old Austin and new Austin. It is quintessential east Austin... huge patio, live music, food truck in the back slinging killer food... but inside there's a quiet sophistication, and you're just as likely to be introduced to a classic cock- tail you'd never had as grabbing a round of Shiners.

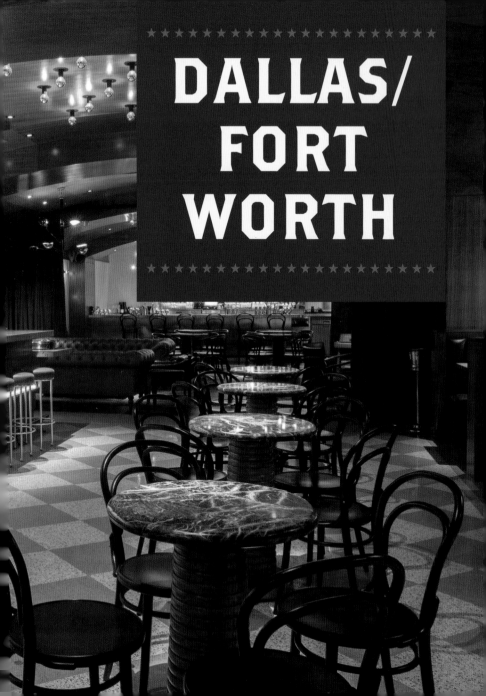

DALLAS/
FORT
WORTH

★ ★

"THERE IS NO SUCH THING AS TOO MUCH GOOD WHISKEY."

—Mark Twain

Dallas... oh Dallas... I'm from DFW (more specifically the FW part, but I live in Dallas and have for the majority of my adult life) and I can honestly say that it's one of the most fun cocktail scenes in the United States. We have record stores with cocktail bars in them, we have a food truck park that's rocking a Jason Kosmas program, and we have cocktails bars that should be considered among the best in the world. The Dallas/Fort Worth scene is a microcosm of what the Texas cocktail scene represents. It's the epitome of diversity. From the college town of Denton having its own burgeoning scene 45 minutes north of Dallas and Fort Worth, to the great programs in the fine dining restaurants of Dallas, to the suburban surge of the craft scene, to Brad Hensarling singlehandedly dragging Fort Worth into the cocktail renaissance... DFW is not only its own thing, but it's also everything.

My favorite hidden aside from the DFW story is the Arcadia Theatre. While Lucky Campbell (the man who would turn Bolsa into a powerhouse, start The Chesterfield with Michael Martensen, and is the current owner of Parliament) was working at The Club in the Centrum building, he was approached about a project to redo the Arcadia Theater. This was 2006 when cocktails were basically only in NYC. As part of the project, the owner of the building flew Lucky to NYC to meet the man he'd be working with on the menu, Dale DeGroff.

The Arcadia burned to the ground on June 21st, 2006. Oh, what could have been...

★ ★

GRAPEFRUIT THYME CORDIAL

- 2 ruby red grapefruits
- 2 large lemons
- Handful of thyme

Peel and juice 2 ruby red grapefruits and juice 2 large lemons. Save grapefruit peels. Add equal parts juice and equal parts sugar and stir slowly over low heat with about a handful of thyme. Let that simmer covered for about 30 minutes to bring out grapefruit flavor but do not let it burn. Cool down and store.

— PALOMA REYNA —

Bolsa
614 W Davis St
Dallas, TX 75208
(214) 367-9367
bolsadallas.com

Bolsa started the farm-to-table revolution in Dallas. They were the first restaurant to outwardly focus on fresh ingredients and this was not just in the kitchen, but also behind the bar. The beginning of the program was Eddie "Lucky" Campbell's big entrance on the scene, another Dallas OG who owns and runs Parliament now. With some of the most important bartenders in Dallas spending time there (Jason Kosmas, Lucky Campbell, Kyle Hilla, and more) Bolsa, is still cranking out one of the best programs in the city. The Paloma Reyna is a pretty straightforward Paloma with a touch of thyme. It's as refreshing as it sounds. The grapefruit thyme cordial is also great with gin or vodka, so make plenty.

Glassware: **Collins Glass**
Garnish: **Orange Peel, Thyme Sprig**

- **1.5 oz tequila**
- **.75 oz grapefruit thyme cordial**
- **.5 oz lime juice**

1. Combine ingredients in a shaker with ice and shake vigorously.

2. Strain into a collins glass, filled with ice.

3. Top with Topo Chico.

— GRAPES OF WRATH —

Thompson's Bookstore
900 Houston St
Fort Worth, TX 76102
(817) 882-8003

thompsonsbookstore.com

Thompson's Bookstore in Downtown Fort Worth is quite proud of their history. While the bar opened in 2015, the building was a part of Hell's Half Acre. This was Fort Worth's red light district in the 1800's. In 1910, the building was turned into a pharmacy, then a coffee company, then a pharmacy again until 1973, when it became a bookstore. Today, it's a two story bar, the top being the bookstore and the bottom a speakeasy that feels like a pharmacy. If the blue light is on and you know the password, you're welcome in for a tasty libation. This particular one uses Fort Worth's own TX Whiskey.

Glassware: **Rocks Glass**
Garnish: **Orange Wheel, Cherry**

- 1.75 oz TX Blended Whiskey
- .75 oz simple syrup
- .75 oz lemon juice
- 1 oz egg white
- .75 oz Chateau Ste. Michelle syrah

1. Reverse dry shake the first four ingredients and fine strain into a rocks glass.

2. Add ice and float syrah on top.

3. Garnish with an orange half wheel and a cherry.

~ WHITE ROCK WITCH ~

Armoury D.E.
2714 Elm St
Dallas, TX 75226
(972) 803-5151
armouryde.com

When they saw an old sign stenciled on the inside brick wall, Armoury D.E. knew they had their name. Since 2015, Armoury has been a vital part of the Dallas scene, and is part of the Deep Ellum triangle, along with Black Swan Saloon and High & Tight. If you're looking for a never-ending supply of cocktails with three distinct vibes, this is your spot. Barman Chad Yarborough has created one of the most respected programs in the city and one of the most creative menus you'll see in the state. This is a bittersweet yet bright cocktail with strong herbal notes from the hills of Texas.

Glassware: **Highball Glass**
Garnish: **Orange Zest**

- • 1.5 oz Devils River whiskey
- • .75 oz Amico amaro
- • .75 oz lemon
- • .75 oz cappilaire syrup

1. Combine ingredients in a shaker with ice and shake vigorously.

2. Strain into a highball glass.

3. Garnish with orange zest.

—Western Son Distillery—

If you're a small Texas town, like Pilot Point (50 miles north of Dallas,) when a distillery opens in your town, it's a pretty big deal. Western Son started in an industrial area outside of Dallas, but they grew so quickly that they had to uproot the entire operation and they landed in Pilot Point.

They secured a 30,000 sq. ft. building just 300 yards from the downtown square and five minutes from Lake Ray Roberts. The new location has a live music stage, massive front patio, beautiful tasting room, and lounge. They also upgraded their distilling equipment, including the addition of an Artisan Still Designed 650 gallon pot still.

Western Son has also started brewing beer, under the name Whistle Post Brewing Company. The idea was to create an experience that anyone could enjoy. With rotating BBQ trailers and food trucks, Saturdays at Western Son have become an event. Ta dah! Vodka/Whiskey Tourism!

Funny note… the nickname of the building is "The Old Panty Factory." Built in the 1960s, during the 70s and 80s the Russell-Newman Clothing Company and their primary products were bikini bottoms, briefs, and lingerie. Instead of getting their panties in a wad, Western Son embraced this history and made one of the bathrooms a shrine to commemorate the building's historic past. On one wall reads a quote from a local resident, "My mother-in-law worked here and my father-in-law worked at the GM seat upholstery factory. He used to say they were both in the seat covering business."

Western Son Distillery manufactures Western Vodka, Western Son Gin, and Red River Whiskey, including Red River Bourbon and is distributed in over 20 states across the United States.

Western Son
217 W Division St
Pilot Point, TX 76258
(940) 324-0008
westernsondistillery.com

This is one of the house cocktails you can try when you head to Pilot Point to visit the distillery. It's a pretty awesome time.

Glassware: **Rocks Glass**

- 2 oz Western Son blueberry vodka
- 1 oz simple syrup
- 1 oz fresh lemon juice

1. Combine ingredients in a shaker with ice and shake vigorously.

2. Strain into a rocks glass.

3. Float pinot noir on top.

Pisco, in case you aren't familiar, is a brandy distilled from grape-like cognac. However, to be called pisco, the spirit must be made from grapes grown in specific areas of Peru and Chile and distilled to proof. It works as a great gin substitution in negronis and gimlets. My favorite available in the United States is Campo de Encanto's Grand and Noble Pisco, but if it's not available, Pisco Porton should be and it's fabulous.

OLGA BREESKIN

Bottled in Bond
Recipe: Hector Zavala
5285 Dallas Pkwy Ste. 420
Frisco, TX 75034
(469) 731-5410

bottledinbondparlour.com

Named after the Bottled in Bond Act of 1897, Bottled in Bond is a great example of how cocktail culture is moving into the suburbs. Suburban areas like Frisco near Dallas, or Clear Lake near Houston, typically have plenty of farm-to-table restaurants, but cocktail-driven beverage programs are fairly new. They are the future, my friends. After training in the city centers, the suburban cocktails are the next big trend in Texas.

Glassware: **Coupe Glass**
Garnish: **Chile Pepper**

- ◆ **2 oz pisco**
- ◆ **.75 oz lemon**
- ◆ **.75 oz ancho chile demerara**
- ◆ **.5 oz egg white**

1. Combine all ingredients and dry shake without ice for 10 seconds.

2. Shake with ice for 30 seconds.

3. Fine mesh strain into a coupe glass.

4. Garnish with a dried chile pepper.

— EVERYBODY'S GIRL —

Lounge Here
Recipe: Brad Bowen
9028 Garland Rd
Dallas, TX 75218
(214) 238-3374

theloungehere.com

This drink is as easy drinking and as laid back as the neighborhood that surrounds this cocktail haven. Brad Bowen's running a fantastic program in this very cool neighborhood setting. This cocktail features Austin's Highborn Dry Gin.

Glassware: **Collins Glass**
Garnish: **Grapefruit Peel**

- .75 oz Highborn Texas Dry Gin
- .75 oz St Germaine
- .75 oz Lustau Fino Sherry
- .75 oz grapefruit
- .25 oz lemon juice
- Top with prosecco

1. Combine ingredients in a shaker with ice and shake vigorously.

2. Strain into a collins glass.

3. Top with prosecco and garnish with a grapefruit peel.

LOUNGE HERE

Let's continue the neighborhood trend, shall we? Lounge Here is one of the coolest-looking bars you'll ever encounter. It's kind of a cross between West Texas and Palm Springs, with obvious nods to both vast deserts and 70s airport lounges... in a great way. It's becoming an East Dallas staple, which thrills me since I live here and we were in need of some killer libations in this part of town.

—Cocktail Enthusiast—

Kevin Gray is a Native Texan who headed off to the East Coast and fell in love with cocktails. His website, Cocktail Enthusiast, is one of the most influential cocktail-based media outlets in the United States and he's based here in Texas. I had a chance to chat with him about his entry into this whole cocktail thing...

When did you start Cocktail Enthusiast?

2009. I had just recently discovered good drinks. Cocktail Enthusiast was my creative (and healthier) outlet for exploring that newfound interest.

Where did the interest in cocktails come from?

I've always loved to eat. Not just for sustenance, but for sport. Give me the best, weirdest, most unique thing you've got, and I want to eat it. So it was pretty easy to apply that same attitude toward drinks, especially as bars began to approach cocktails with more of a culinary- and craft-based mindset.

How is the cocktail landscape different on the coasts than it is in Texas?

The craft cocktail movement really began on the coasts, New York and San Francisco in particular. As it trickled its way into Texas, the community here embraced better drinks. But we're still playing from behind, both in bar and consumer adoption. In some ways, that can be frustrating, but in another very tangible way, it's exciting. There's still so much to explore here, whether it's playing with interesting spirits or getting a vodka soda drinker to try his first gateway cocktail that will pique his interest in good drinks.

Over the past decade, the number of bars in Texas serving craft cocktails has expanded dramatically. Before, you knew of one or two bars in each major city, and you'd have to ask for a particular bartender you could trust. Now, good drinking has been normalized, and

not just at the fancy cocktail-centric bars. These days, you've got a good chance of finding a well-made Negroni on the menu of a downtown bistro, and a perfectly stirred Sazerac at a suburban steakhouse. Hell, even a lot of sports bars can make you a decent Old Fashioned now.

What are your current projects?

I'm currently leading the editorial charge at Bevvy, which is the San Francisco-based parent company of Cocktail Enthusiast. Aside from that, I'm contributing boozy stories for a variety of magazines, and visiting as many distilleries and bars as I can. It's a fun job. And while the well-stocked liquor cabinet is a nice perk, the best part about covering this industry is meeting all the hardworking people behind these products and places.

Okay, last one... what immediately comes to mind when I say the phrase "Texas Cocktails?"

Texas cocktails can be as diverse as the state itself. We're largely influenced by our neighbors to the south, but Texas draws residents from all over the country and the world, and our cocktail scene reflects that fact. That said, a true "Texas cocktail" might include ingredients indigenous to the region (there's nothing better than a perfectly ripe Texas-grown grapefruit or peach) and one of our many and constantly increasing local spirits.

⏤ SUMMER ON THE RIVIERA ⏤

Proper
Recipe: Lisa Little-Adams, Proper 2014
409 W Magnolia Ave
Fort Worth, TX 76104
(817) 984-1133

Proper is on one of the most happening streets in Fort Worth, Magnolia. They are a contemporary cocktail bar with a comfortable atmosphere inside and a quaint patio for relaxing under the stars with your pups and your pals. They're another example of great cocktails in Fort Worth. Fort Worth, in my opinion, is the most underrated cocktail scene in Texas. Not nearly enough attention is paid to my home town, and I promise you that the drinks in Cowtown rival any in the state. This summery drink is a riff on a gin sour and is as crowd pleasing as a good honky-tonk band at Billy Bob's on a Friday night.

Glassware: **Coupe Glass**
Garnish: **Lemon Twist**

- • 2 oz Citadell gin
- • .5 oz Bitter Truth elderflower liquor
- • .5 oz lemon juice
- • .5 oz Ferrand dry curacao
- • .25 oz simple syrup

1. Combine ingredients in a shaker with ice and shake vigorously.

2. Strain into a coupe glass.

3. Garnish with a lemon twist.

— Black Swan Saloon —

2708 ELM ST
DALLAS, TX 75226
(214) 749-4848
BLACKSWANSALOON.COM

What's the most important thing to remember if you open your own bar? If you're one of the nicest guys in the city, no one cares if the cups are plastic. Gabe Sanchez came from the humblest of beginnings, running VIP tables at $10K a pop in Vegas. "It was a 24-hour job. When you came to Vegas and you had a lot of money, I'd take care of you. Cart you around, make sure you have a good time, make sure it stays between you and your buddies. That sort of thing. It was a grind, dude."

Gabe had just graduated from the F&B program at UNLV and was approached to do the same thing at the infamous Ghost Bar on top of the W Hotel in Dallas. He saw it as an opportunity to experience a new city and get the heck out of Vegas for a while. Four years later, he found himself on a trip to Deep Ellum with friends Clint and Whitney Barlow, who were looking to re-open the iconic Dallas music venue, Trees. He found himself eyeballing the empty storefront directly across the street and, shortly thereafter, Black Swan Saloon was born.

There's no sign at Black Swan Saloon. This was a calculated decision. You could call it a speakeasy if you want, but it's certainly not fronted by a candy shop or taqueria. Gabe made the decision to skip signage when he visited Daddy's in LA (now closed), which didn't have a sign and was pretty difficult to randomly stumble upon. He told me, "We walked in and no one looked towards the door. That was different… Everyone who was in there knew someone. There was a reason they were there. I loved that idea. It worked because I tend to have a big personality and everyone's a homie to me and I was so stoked when people would walk in the door."

Black Swan Saloon, to me, represents everything that the Texas cocktail community is about. Service, simplicity, and having a good time. Black Swan's a bar. No more, no less, just a bar. Don't get me wrong, Gabe's cocktails are pretty stellar and he owns one of Texas' OG cocktail bars, but he's far more interested in you as a person and a guest than bamboozling you with tinctures. Black Swan, much like many of the other best cocktail bars in Texas, is service first, drinks second.

Gabe told me, "If you treat people right and they have a sense of ownership in a place and are there as it grows, they're a lot more willing to try new things." That, my friends, is how you grow a cocktail scene and that is how you become one of the most loved and trusted bartenders in Texas. His drink, the True Romance, will have you smiling as much as Gabe himself.

— TRUE ROMANCE —

Black Swan Saloon
Recipe: Gabe Sanchez, Owner, Black Swan Saloon

A Gabe Sanchez original, this is a boozy, smoky libation that is delightfully bitter with a hint of sweetness.

Glassware: **Rocks Glass**
Garnish: **Lime Zest**

- **1.5 oz mezcal**
- **1 oz yellow chartreuse**
- **.75 oz Averna**

1. Stir all ingredients in a glass.

2. Serve with a big rock, pinch of sea salt, and lime zest.

—D&D Shrubs—
and Syrups

DDSHRUBSNSYRUPS.COM

Chris Dempsey's desire to make the best shrubs in Texas started when he was working in the beverage program at the Four Seasons in Las Colinas, just outside of Dallas. There he met his business partner, Chef Brandon Drew, who started using his shrubs in his cooking and told Chris that he should sell them. After a few of his regulars said the same thing, he started thinking about the lack of quality mixers on the market made with fresh ingredients.

In December of 2015, Brandon and Chris started D&D Shrubs and Syrups and now make 16 core flavors. The Blackberry Shrub, was an essential element in the cocktail that propelled Chris to the National Finals of the Copper & Kings Mixt&pe Cocktail Competition.

If you are in Dallas, you can find D&D at various events, including every weekend at the Dallas Farmers Market,and also purchase products on their website. Chris was cool enough to provide us with two shrub recipes... the right one and the fast one.

How to Make Blackberry Beet Shrub (the Right One)

Cold press 1 lb blackberries
Cold press 1 lb beets. These should give you between 28-34oz juice each.
Add 30 oz organic Apple Cider Vinegar.
You should have a total of 64 oz liquid. To this add 25 oz honey to sweeten. For longer shelf life, add 2 tbsp citric acid. Strain and bottle. Store in cool, dark place or refrigerate up to one year. Flavors will mellow over time, so the sooner you use it the better it is.

How to Make a Shrub Quickly (the Fast One)

1 lb fruit
1 cup sugar or honey
1 cup organic apple cider vinegar
Put all into a pot and bring to a light boil; simmer until berries burst. Turn off heat and let sit for 15 minutes. Fine strain and bottle.

— CLEAN-CUT-KID —

Hide
Recipe: Scott Jenkins, John Ruiz, Trey Buquoi
2816 Elm St
Dallas, TX 75226
(214) 396-8050
hide.bar

When Hide in Dallas opened, it immediately rivaled every other cocktail bar in the area. Their use of technology and gastronomy allows a different level of creativity than most other bars in Texas. Head Barman Scott Jenkins is a self-taught cocktail nerd who took a specific liking to Dave Arnold's (Liquid Intelligence) style and decided to base his program on molecular mixology. Innovative, yet approachable, Hide is an experience that feels like it could live in any city in the world. The Clean-Cut-Kid is one of their simple cocktails... namely because I didn't feel like writing "now go buy a centrifuge" in any of the recipe directions.

Glassware: **Cocktail Glass**
Garnish: **Lemon Peel**

- **2.5 oz rye whiskey (90% or above rye mash)**
- **.375 oz Suze**
- **2 dashes black walnut bitters**
- **.25 oz Solera-aged Coconut-White balsamic vinegar**
- **3 dashes lemon-coriander tincture**

1. Stir all ingredients.

2. Strain into a chilled cocktail glass.

3. Express a lemon peel over the top and serve.

— Herman Marshall —

Fifteen years ago at a neighborhood coffee shop, a small group of friends would gather on weekends for coffee. Nobody really remembers when whiskey became the subject of debate, but once it did nothing else was discussed with the same intensity. Over the next four years all the ideas and plans for a Texas distillery were put to paper.

When a tightknit group of friends with mutual interests come together to start a project, every now and then, you have a perfect storm of overlapping talents and resources that meld into something truly special. Or the other ten dudes bail. That's when Herman Beckley and Marshall Louis's partnership solidified. They had the plans, but now, they needed to start making whiskey.

Marshall hails from a winemaking family from Cape Town, South Africa, and Herman, from the corn belt of Indiana. With their powers combined, they created a line of whiskeys that rival anything in the state. Even so, the whiskeys were under the Texas radar until their bourbon took a silver medal at the 2013 American Distilling Institute's Spirit Competition. "That's when the distributors started paying attention and wanted to sign us up," said Russel Louis, Herman Marshall's VP.

From the beginning, Herman and Marshall have been set on adhering to the historical methods of production. "We make very simple uncomplicated recipes, with very simple, uncomplicated technique, which is how whiskeys was made in the late 1700s and early 1800s," said Herman. Most of the corn for their bourbon and single-malt whiskies is grown in the McKinney area, with supplemental harvests coming from the Texas Panhandle. And their rye and barley comes from North Dakota. Herman Marshall is available statewide.

PINK CAMPARI

Herman Marshall
803 Shepherd Dr
Garland, TX 75042
(469) 298-3903

dallasdistilleries.com

This is a great balance of bitter and sweet. The Campari pairs beautifully with the spiciness of the Herman Marshall rye.

Glassware: **Martini Glass**
Garnish: **Raspberries, Lime Twist**

- 1 oz Campari
- 1 oz HM rye whiskey
- 4-5 fresh raspberries
- Splash of pear and cranberry juices
- Splash of sweet and sour mix

1. Combine ingredients in a shaker with ice and shake vigorously.

2. Strain into a chilled martini glass.

3. Garnish with skewered raspberries and lime twist.

⚔ APPLE BLOSSOM ⚔

Industry Alley
Recipe: Charlie Papenceo
1711 S Lamar St
Dallas, TX 75215
(214) 238-3111
industryalley.com

Industry Alley is the latest bar from Dallas' Godfather of cocktails, Charlie Papenceo, Pap for short. This is a bartenders' bar through and through. Pony of High Life? Oh hell yes. Sazerac, yep, and it's better than the one you make. Shot of Angostura? Fine, but we're doing bourbon first. This is where you go to meet the bartenders you'll soon be sitting in front of, ordering fizzes and daisies and flips (oh my). Charlie's an old-school New Jersey guy who ended up in Dallas but decided to keep making the same drinks he did back home. His first bar, Windmill Lounge, was one of the most influential in town before Charlie left it to start Industry Alley. He's the quintessential bartender and Texas is lucky he's with us now.

Glassware: **Collins Glass**

- **1.5 oz Applejack**
- **.5 oz St. Germaine**
- **.5 oz lime juice**

1. Add all ingredients to a collins glass.

2. Stir and top with seltzer water.

Jettison
Recipe: George Kaiho
1878 Sylvan Avenue
Dallas, TX 75208
(214) 238-2643

Jettison is a project brought forth by the good people at Houndstooth Coffee. When Jettison was opening, part of the concept of the bar was to do a coffee-influenced cocktail, using coffee as a part of the cocktail but not as the dominant ingredient. According to bar manager George Kaiho, "This cocktail started from a concept of cognac as a base with coffee, amaro, and orgeat involved. As I tried the combination, I liked it more with Amaro, Lucano and less cognac, and eventually the ratio flipped, being Lucano as a base and cognac to support the alcohol." George also won an Amaro Lucano cocktail competition with this recipe. Try this and you'll understand why.

Glassware: **Coupe Glass**
Garnish: **Star Anise**

- 1.25 oz Amaro Lucano
- .75 oz Hennessy VS cognac
- .25 oz Pierre Ferrand dry curacao
- .25 oz lemon juice
- .5 oz house orgeat (from real almonds)
- .75 oz uncut cold brew coffee from Houndstooth Coffee
- Dash Paychaud's bitters

1. Combine ingredients in a shaker with ice and shake vigorously.

2. Fine strain into a coupe glass and garnish with torched star anise.

Thumper is the nickname given to the watermelon in Texas. Texas watermelons, like the mighty grape fruit, are some of the best on the planet. Bite into one and you'll understand why it's one of Texas' largest crops.

— 1000W THUMPER —

Midnight Rambler
1530 Main St
Dallas, TX 75201
(214) 261-4601

midnightramblerbar.com

Midnight Rambler is one of the sexist places you'll ever see. I can't think of a better way to describe the feeling you get when you enter the Joule Hotel, descend down the stairs, past the neon "cocktails" sign, into the coolest cocktail den in Texas. Chad Solomon and Christy Pope oversee the program and Midnight Rambler was their second entry in to the Dallas scene, having consulted on the original menus for Victor Tangos, one of the first cocktail programs in Dallas. While not from Dallas, these Sasha Petraske proteges now make their home here and are two of the coolest cats you'll ever meet.

Glassware: **Collins Glass**
Garnish: **Watermelon Spear**

- .75 oz fresh lime juice
- .5 oz mineral simple (1 part Crazy Water #4: 1 part sugar)
- 2 oz fresh watermelon juice
- 1.5 oz Tanqueray
- 1 dash Angostura bitters
- 2 drops mineral aaline (1 part kosher salt: 9 parts Crazy Water #4)
- 2 drops Electric Matcha (can substitute Vieux Pontarlier Absinthe)

1. Combine ingredients in a shaker with ice and shake vigorously.

2. Strain into a collins glass.

3. Top with ice-cold club soda.

~ BURNT SAGE SOUR ~

Standard Pour
2900 McKinney Ave
Dallas, TX 75204
(214) 935-1370

tspdallas.com

The Standard Pour is the bar that you go to in Dallas to find out which bars you need to go to in Dallas. The bartenders that have come through their program are some of the best in the state. Co-founder Brian McCullough is one of the most influential bartenders in Dallas, and his consulting and event work, is one of the reasons that the cocktail scene in North Texas has blossomed. When you look at the Burnt Sage Sour, the first thing you notice a pretty large amount of Ancho Reyes. This is a wonderful spirit made from Ancho chiles. Brian said, "It has a vast array of cocktail applications aside from just being delicious by itself. So it is a natural evolution for this to be a Texas favorite amongst us cocktail folks." Toss in some overproof rum and you have yourself a splendid sour. This also works well with agave spirits.

Glassware: **Nick & Nora**
Garnish: **Sage Leaf**

* 1 oz Ancho Reyes
* 1 oz Plantation O.F.T.D. rum
* 1 oz pineapple juice
* .5 oz lime juice
* 1 oz burnt sugar syrup
* 3 sage leaves

1. Shake all ingredients, saving one sage leaf for garnish, and double strain into Nick and Nora glass.

2. Place sage on top and simply brulee the sage leaf on top of cocktail (flame the sage leaves briefly with butane torch—be careful!).

⚊ CARDS ON THE TABLE ⚊

Proof & Pantry
1722 Routh St
Dallas, TX 75201
(214) 880-9940
proofandpantry.com

Located in the middle of one of the largest privately funded arts districts in the country, Proof & Pantry is a multi-faceted American restaurant and bar featuring progressive, yet approachable fare. Michael Martensen and his squad have created a program to rival any bar in the city. The cocktail menu is organized by No Proof, Low Proof, and High Proof, so you can choose the path you're feeling that evening. The Cards on the Table is a simple tequila sour, but with the addition of fruity and herbaceous notes only slightly masked by the cracked black pepper.

Glassware: **Coupe Glass**
Garnish: **Cracked Black Pepper**

- **2 oz strawberry infused blanco tequila**
- **.75 oz lemon juice**
- **.75 oz simple syrup**
- **2 dashes cardamom tincture**

1. Combine ingredients in a shaker with ice and shake vigorously.

2. Strain into a coupe glass.

~ THE SMOKING GUN ~

Parliament is an uptown Dallas neighborhood cocktail bar that doubles as an industry haunt. It churns out talented bartender after talented bartender and will be important to this city for years to come. This is an impressive cocktail to serve, and once you start smoking cocktails, be careful, because it's awfully addicting. This is a Lucky Campbell original and it's fabulous.

Glassware: **Old Fashioned Glass**
Garnish: **Luxardo Cherries**

- .5 oz orgeat syrup
- 3 dashes Angostura bitters
- 1 orange peel squeezed to release the oils into the mix
- .5 oz water
- 2 oz vanilla infused bourbon
- .5 oz Averna Amaro

1. Stir all ingredients and pour into a decanter. Smoke with cherry wood. Swirl to infuse smoke into cocktail.

2. Slowly pour over a large piece of ice in an old fashioned glass.

3. Garnish with Luxardo cherries.

—Parliament—

2418 ALLEN ST
DALLAS, TX 75204
(469) 804-4321
PARLIAMENTDALLAS.COM

Eddie "Lucky" Campbell is one of the pillars of the Dallas cocktail community. Lucky is one of the first people in Dallas to help spark the city's path towards the cocktail Renaissance. After starting things at Bolsa, Lucky moved into a partnership with Micheal Martensen and created The Chesterfield. Over a hundred drinks on the menu, very focused on craft, and one of the first times Dallas had a bar open specifically to serve craft cocktails. It's since gone, but his new project, Parliament, has the same progressive spirit. Lucky's eye for innovation lives here and it's one of the best in town.

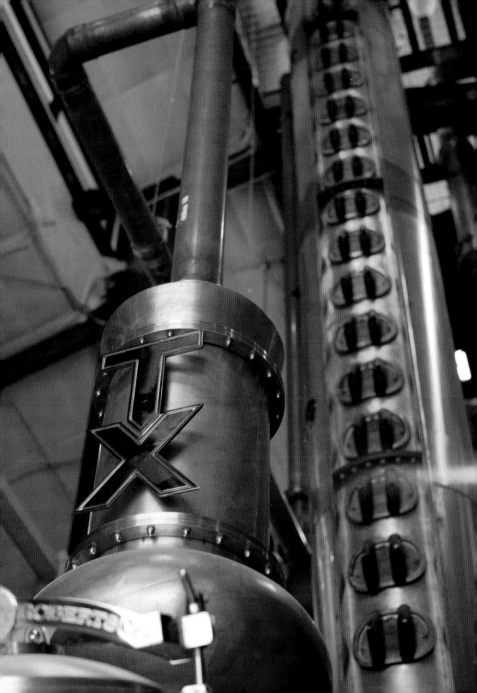

— Firestone and Robertson —

Founded in 2010 by Leonard Firestone and Troy Robertson, Firestone and Robinson Distilling Company is responsible for giving the world TX Whiskey. F&R released TX Blended Whiskey in June of 2012. TX is a blend of sourced whiskeys, however, in December of 2016, F&R released their TX Straight Bourbon, which is a thoroughly Texas made bourbon... It's badass.

The blended whiskey was awarded "Best American Craft Whiskey" at the 2013 San Francisco World Spirits Competition, and I'm sure the bourbon will end up with similar accolades. Their original location is in Fort Worth in a revitalized pre-Prohibition warehouse just south of downtown. But hold your horses, my friends... this new Whiskey Ranch they built... good gracious, it's amazing.

They bought a country club that overlooks downtown Fort Worth and stuck a $17 million distillery and visitor's center in the middle of the golf course that Ben Hogan and Byron Nelson used to caddy. I KNOW, RIGHT? Glen Gardens Country Club was built in 1912, and F&R is preserving the grounds, and maintaining the golf course, which is only available for friends, family, and the occasional charity events. Whiskey Ranch will be the largest distillery west of the Mississippi River and will also use a 45-foot copper column still in full view of visitors. This is the type of place that will bring whiskey tourism to Fort Worth. Seriously. It's the bees knees.

When discussing the new TX Straight Bourbon, Firestone said, "This is Texas corn, Texas wheat, Texas water, Texas climate, and our Texas yeast." Head distiller, Rob Arnold, gathered samples of yeast from all over North Texas and then took them to TCU for a DNA analysis. They wound up choosing the one from the pecan nut on a friend's ranch... sounds about right.

Both whiskeys are available in Texas and in a growing number of states throughout the United States in most major liquor stores.

— TEXAS GENTLEMAN —

Firestone & Robertson
901 W Vickery Blvd
Fort Worth, TX 76104
(817) 840-9140

frdistilling.com

This will warm you up with some TX Whiskey and pep you up with Austin's own Caffe Del Fuego. Think of this as a coffee old fashioned.

Glassware: **Rocks Glass**
Garnish: **Orange Peel**

- **2 oz TX blended whiskey**
- **.5 oz Caffe Del Fuego**
- **3 dashes Fee Brothers Aztec Chocolate bitters**

1. Combine whiskey, Caffe Del Fuego, and bitters in a rocks glass over ice.

2. Garnish with an orange peel.

~ THE FLEUR DU MAL ~

Paschall Bar
122 N Locust St
Denton, TX 76201

Paschall Bar is cocktail bar in a college town in Denton, TX. I couldn't believe it myself the first time I walked in. Owned collectively by the band Midlake, Paschall Bar is the hippest spot in a town that's known as one of the hippest towns in Texas. The cocktail, named after Charles Baudelaire's volume of poetry—"Les Fleurs du Mal" or "The Flowers of Evil"—is a riff on a Corpse Reviver #2. Elegant, sexy, and inviting, the Fleur du Mal was originally a Valentine feature crafted for the lonely hearts at The Paschall Bar; since then, it's become one of their most beloved and endeared cocktails.

Glassware: **Coupe Glass**
Garnish: **Dried Rose Buds**

- 1 oz gin
- 1 oz Lillet Blanc
- 1 oz St. Germain
- .5 oz lemon juice
- .5 oz grapefruit juice
- .25 oz grenadine
- .25 oz Kina Tonic

1. Shake and double strain into a coupe glass.

2. Spritz with orange blossom water.

3. Garnish with dried rose buds.

~ SOUTHERN SHIPWRECK ~

Rapscallion
2023 Greenville Ave #110
Dallas, TX 75206
(469) 291-5660

dallasrapscallion.com

Built to be a beautiful addition to the Lower Greenville neighborhood, Rapscallion is one of the best programs in town. As they say, it's "creative, expansive, but not expensive." Their beverage director, Eddie Eakin, is one of Dallas' most interesting curators of spirits and pretty innovative with their big batch program. Make sure you check out their by-request-only tiki menu. The Southern Shipwreck has a bit of a tiki vibe to it and the combination of navy strength rum and the slight sweetness of the TX Whiskey makes this drink a bold yet refreshing experience.

Glassware: **Coupe Glass**
Garnish: **Sugar**

- 1 oz Smith and Cross
- 1 oz TX whiskey
- .75 oz lime
- .75 oz orgeat
- .25 oz brown sugar syrup
- 5 dashes Scrappys chocolate bitters

1. Combine ingredients in a shaker with ice and shake vigorously.

2. Strain into a sugar-rimmed coupe glass.

AVIATION VARIATION

Bird Café
155 E 4th St
Fort Worth, TX 76102
(817) 332-2473
birdinthe.net

Once called "The Only Blue Cocktail You Should Ever Order" by Gothamist, the Aviation is one of the most important cocktails in this little cocktail renaissance of ours. It first appeared in print in *Recipes for Mixed Drinks* in 1916 by Hugo Ensslin from the Hotel Wallick in New York City, and it more famously appeared in *The Savoy Cocktail Book* by Harry Craddock. In the early 2000s, the Aviation was seen as a secret handshake for bartenders in the know. This variation from the Bird Café in Fort Worth's beautiful Sundance Square is like creating a flip based on the Aviation.

Glassware: **Coupe Glass**
Garnish: **Rosebuds**

- 1.5 oz Ford's gin
- .75 oz Parfait Amour
- .25 oz Luxardo Maraschino
- .75 oz lemon juice
- .25 oz simple syrup
- 2 dash lavender bitters
- 2 drop rosewater
- 1 egg white

1. Put all ingredients into pint glass. Add ice.

2. Reverse dry shake until egg white is very frothy.

3. Top with a pinch of crushed rosebuds and one single rosebud in the middle of the coupe glass.

— A CONVERSATION WITH —
Michael Martensen

You started at The Mansion in 2007. How was the reception to these drinks?

I had the wealthiest people in Texas walking in and ordering Miller Lite. Did I want to have Miller Lite? No. But the people paying my bills were the people drinking Miller Lite. I had to re-train some people but overall, everyone was 100% all-in. I did get a little bit crazy, midway in when I was feeling it like, "Oh yes, I'm killing it. I'm going to put 10 ingredients to this cocktail now. Look at how great this cocktail is." I was young and stupid. Those cocktails didn't last long.

How did your approach to making drinks change because of being in Texas?

Of course, not being from Texas, we all have a perception of Texas. In my mind, I have three drinks that will always be there... tequila, champagne (because it's a fancy), and I like the idea of using both spice and peach because we're in Texas.

The reception of Dallas to the bar was amazing. People were coming in. It was hot because there were artists. It was like George Michaels was coming in all the time, and all these affluent people of Dallas that are—Not affluent, I mean they're wealthy but they're also artistically affluent.

It's the cool kids with social collateral.

It's the cool kids, and so there's all kinds of stuff going on. The head bartender at The Mansion really is the key to a city. You can make somebody's trip to Dallas so much more if they're open to it, and I love that part about Dallas. I love that it's a big enough city but small enough town to get things done.

So talk to me about The Cedars Social.

I met Brian Williams within about a year and a half of working that job. Then, we decided to open a place together. We opened up in 2011 and I had just spent almost 3 years going to the best bars all across the US, so I had plenty of ideas.

So, I'm familiar with Dallas and The Cedars, at the time, was not in a good neighborhood. Why did you put that thing there?

Jack Mathews gave us free rent for two years. When you know you don't have to pay rent you can open it up and do something special. If you look at the cocktail world, every single influential cocktail bar has been in the ghetto. Milk and Honey, Bourbon & Branch, Tenderloin, Violet Hour... all in bad parts of town.

To you, what is a Texas cocktail?

A Texas cocktail, I've actually thought about this and this is what I do enjoy about Texas drinking and Texas cocktail. We all know East and West Coast are the biggest influencers of the modern American Cocktail, East-West coast, what Texas is to me is the Third Coast. You've got McAllen growing ridiculous citrus and the best grapefruits in the world. Then, you've got this whole whiskey component that Texas has become very good at. You've also got some of the most amazing spirits in the world just south of us. And you tie that up into a Texas atmosphere which is true southern hospitality. And we're influenced by it all. A Texas cocktail is Americana.

— BLESSING OF AGAVE —

Shoals Sound and Service
2614 Elm St Ste 110
Dallas, Texas
(972) 808-6976

Shoals is open. It was a long process, full of temporary licenses and hosting pop ups, but it's done, it's here, and Omar Yeefoon and Michael Martensen now run one of the coolest spots in town. Shoals is one of the most-stripped down, straightforward bars they've ever collaborated on. Shoals is classics, done perfectly, no bullshit. Shoals feels like you've found yourself in Omar's living room. He's playing records (his call, not yours) and being the consummate host. It's relaxed and cool and a very easy place to be. You can order whatever you want at Shoals, but the menu is just classic cocktails. I did convince Omar to contribute an original recipe, however. This flip is Texas in a glass.

Glassware: **Coupe Glass**
Garnish: **Grapefruit Peel**

- **1.5 oz Tequila Cabeza**
- **.5 oz aperol**
- **.75 oz fresh grapefruit**
- **.25 oz lime juice**
- **.5 oz agave syrup**
- **Egg white**

1. Combine all ingredients and dry shake without ice for 10 seconds.

2. Shake with ice for 30 seconds.

3. Fine mesh strain into a coupe glass.

4. Garnish with a grapfruit peel.

— Trigger's Toys —

Trigger's Toys was started by Bryan Townsend when he was newly unemployed and looking for more of a purpose. His life changed when he decided to head to the hospital with his newly trained puppy, Trigger. That's where he met a nurse who introduced him and Trigger to a little girl who wasn't communicating with others very well. On a whim, Bryan suggested she give Trigger a treat. She did.

Then Bryan suggested the little girl follow Trigger through a tunnel. She did. "Her mother told me that it was the first time she'd ever crawled," Bryan said. It was in that moment that Bryan knew he needed to do something bigger and he never wanted to go another year without helping those he felt he could. Trigger's Toys was born.

The primary fundraising event for Trigger's Toys is The Ultimate Cocktail Experience. In fact, it's one of the largest cocktail-based fundraisers in the nation. In 2016, the event raised more than $200,000 and in 2017 they topped $230,000.

The event is, frankly, amazing. It's built around six unique bar concepts and features more than 35 different cocktails. You have a chance to have some of the best drinks from some of the best bartenders across the state of Texas and beyond. "Through the Ultimate Cocktail Experience, we're proud to offer our community a unique way to experience the talents of our service industry while giving back to an organization that is near and dear to our hearts," said Bryan. "We're so thankful to the bar and restaurant industry, as well as the brands, donors, and friends who will gather together to enjoy great drinks, but most importantly, to support a cause that gives back to hospitalized children and their families."

TL;DR If you want to give to a great cause and do so by drinking some of the best drinks in Texas, the Ultimate Cocktail Experience benefitting Trigger's Toys is the event for you.

—Bar Draught—

(214) 228-4088
BARDRAUGHT.COM

I'd be remiss if I didn't talk about my own company, because I genuinely believe that we're about to change the craft cocktail industry. A few years back, when my favorite cocktail was a "Jim Beam on the rocks," my business partner, Adrian Verdin, and I created and produced a TV pilot about craft cocktails… See, I come from a theatre/film directing background and knew how to tell a story, but didn't know a thing about cocktails. Fast forward to us in LA, at Harvard & Stone, discussing ways we could introduce more people to cocktails by creating an indie music/cocktail festival.

We almost booked The Flaming Lips, we almost booked The Roots, we almost booked Interpol, but nothing seemed to quite work out. But my biggest concern was, "How the hell are we going to serve craft cocktails to 7,000 people anyway?" Adrian told me that he had draft systems at his restaurant and so we started there.

Once we built our first machine, we abandoned the music festival because we could tell the draft cocktail system was the idea we were supposed to run with. Using a combination of our one-of-a kind mobile draft system and our line of all natural, organic mixers, we've created a way for venues to serve craft cocktails in places where it's currently impossible. Ballrooms, stadium concourses, the middle of huge music festivals (see? It all comes full circle), and anywhere that you can't pull off a full cocktail bar. We're damn proud of it and we're damn proud that it was born in Texas. If you ever need to serve a ridiculous amount of cocktails to a ridiculously large group of people, call me.

— HUSK FIZ —

Small Brewpub
333 W Jefferson Blvd
Dallas, TX 75208
(972) 863-1594
smallbrewpub.com

Benj Pocta has always been one of the more underrated bartenders in Dallas. His palate and use of creative ingredients is some of the best in Texas, and Small Brewpub's menu reflects that beautifully. They aren't afraid to use wild yeast and bacteria when it suits them and their barrel program is exciting. On one of the most historic streets in Oak Cliff, Small Brewpub is a hidden gem that deserves more than the moniker of "hidden gem." This Husk Fiz is inspired by George Kappeler's version of the New Orleans Fizz from his book *Modern American Drinks*, printed in 1895. Benj said, "we wanted to keep the affair lactose free for our dairy averse guests, so coconut milk was the perfect choice."

Glassware: **Collins Glass**
Garnish: **Lime Leaf**

- **1.5 oz London Dry-Style gin**
- **.5 oz lime juice**
- **.75 oz coriander syrup**
- **.75 oz coconut milk**
- **Club soda**
- **2 lime leaves (1 for garnish)**
- **Orange blossom water**

1. Shake gin, lime juice, coriander syrup, coconut milk, and torn lime leaf with ice.

2. Strain into a chilled collins glass and top with chilled club soda.

3. Spritz with orange blossom water and garnish with lime leaf.

⇁ SHRUB YOU THE RIGHT WAY ⇀

This was, arguably, the first craft cocktail program in the state, but it was certainly a place that changed cocktails in Texas forever. The great Danny Caffall has been running the bar program for quite a while and this cocktail is a great example of complex flavors while still maintaining approachability.

Glassware: **Rocks Glass**
Garnish: **Lemon Twist**

- 2 oz Maker's Mark bourbon
- .75 oz peach shrub
- .5 oz fresh lemon juice
- .5 oz creme de noyaux
- 1 dash peach bitters

1. Mix all ingredients in shaker tin.

2. Shake and pour.

3. Garnish with mint. You may also top with ginger beer to add a little frizante.

Peach Shrub

Combine peach puree, sugar, and sherry vinegar.

—The Mansion—

2821 TURTLE CREEK BLVD
DALLAS, TX 75219
(214) 443-4747
ROSEWOODHOTELS.COM/EN/MANSION-ON-TURTLE-CREEK-DALLAS/
DINING/MANSION-RESTAURANT

When The Rosewood Mansion was renovated in 2007, it brought with it somewhat of a revolution in the Dallas culinary scene. John Tesar (of Kitchen Confidential fame) took over the reins from Dallas' culinary darling, Dean Fearing. He quickly elevated The Mansion to iconic status, earning one of the only 5 star reviews in Dallas' history. Of course, he also became known as "Dallas' Most Hated Chef," but for our purposes he's a hero. John believes that a bar program is essential to greatness, and when he took over the joint, he brought with him the arrival of Michael Martensen.

So how did you end up deciding that opening up a cocktail bar in Fort Worth, Texas in 2009 was a good idea?

So, there was a girl who really hated the Chat Room, but always came to the Chat Room. One day, she came in and said "I'm gonna open a bar across the street and take all your customers." So I went to my landlord and said "Here's a check for the deposit when it comes up for lease."

So it's 2009, you and I both know that Fort Worth is a whiskey & Coke and beer scene; how was the reception?

Well, no one knew what a cocktail was. For better or worse, we decided not to carry a lot of things. We couldn't do a 7&7 for instance. People around me always preferred a good product, but what I was able to serve them (at the Chat Room) was always subpar. I wanted to fix that.

People started coming to The Usual and started getting great drinks and then they'd go on with their evening. So I'd start getting calls from bartenders at restaurants around town saying "Hey man... what's in this?" I was always liberal with the recipes, but I was always thinking "Dude, you don't have velvet falernum. You can't make it anyway."

And now we have cocktails man! That's it. I'm the one that fell on the sword for it, obviously I'm not the only one, but in this area, in this town... somebody had to at some point. I just decided to be the chump. But it's worked out alright.

—The Usual—

1408 W MAGNOLIA AVE
FORT WORTH, TEXAS
(817) 810-0114

The Usual was the first cocktail-focused bar that opened in North Texas. It would be years after it's opening (in 2009) before anyone in the entire metroplex would try to open anything specifically driven by cocktails.

The Usual is my favorite bar in Texas. I know I'm not supposed to play favorites, but it's been my favorite bar in Texas for damn near ten years now. The Usual, to me, is the perfect balance between innovation and creativity and the relaxed, welcoming, the feeling you get when you've entered your neighborhood dive bar. The program at The Usual singlehandedly dragged Fort Worth, Texas into the cocktail scene. Now if you're opening up a restaurant in Fort Worth, you have to have some sort of cocktail menu. The city expects it, and odds are your first classic cocktail was an Old Fashioned at The Usual.

~ AMBASSADOR PUNSCH ~

About the Ambassador Punsch, Brad told me, "No one orders this drink until they try it, but when they do they're hooked." Swedish Punsch used to be an incredibly important part of many cocktails, but disappeared because of Prohibition.

Glassware: **Coupe Glass**
Garnish: **Lime Wheel**

- 1 oz Zaya rum
- 1 oz Kronan Swedish Punsch
- .5 oz rich simple syrup
- .5 oz lime juice
- 6 drops Elemakule Tiki bitters

1. Combine ingredients in a shaker with ice and shake vigorously.

2. Strain into a coupe glass.

3. Garnish with a lime wheel.

⟞ PEACHY KEANE ⟞

Ida Claire
5001 Belt Line Rd
Dallas, TX 75254
(214) 377-8227

ida-claire.com

I da Claire is built on Southern hospitality. From the same group that created Whiskey Cake and Mexican Sugar, Ida Claire is all about the Southern kitsch. And when you think Southern, you think peaches. This cocktail is named for Margaret D. H. Keane (b. 1927) who was an American artist who mainly painted women, children, and animals, most notably with big eyes. She sold works under her husband's name for years and only received credit after divorcing him.

Glassware: **Rocks Glass**
Garnish: **Dried Peach, Ginger Candy**

- ◆ **1 oz Old Forester bourbon**
- ◆ **.5 oz Giffard Peche de Vigne**
- ◆ **.5 oz King's Ginger Liqueur**
- ◆ **.75 oz honey**
- ◆ **.75 oz lemon juice**
- ◆ **Egg white**

1. Combine all ingredients and dry shake without ice for 10 seconds.

2. Shake with ice for 30 seconds.

3. Fine strain into a rocks glass.

4. Garnish with a dried peach and ginger candy.

— LIPSTICK & ROUGE —

Pie 3.14
2560 King Arthur Blvd #100
Lewisville, TX 75056
(972) 899-2718

pie314everydayeatery.com

Sean Conner is old-school Dallas. The man originally behind the programs at Whiskey Cake and Mexican Sugar left to live that suburban cocktail life when Pie 3.14 was created. He is now in the midst of a series of projects, all in the suburbs of Dallas, Sean is bringing craft cocktail culture to a different demographic than most. Sometimes it's a pizza joint, sometimes it's a taqueria, but it's always serving killer cocktails. The Lipstick & Rouge is what you want on the patio at about 4:45 in the afternoon… once you've dropped all your kids off at soccer and piano lessons.

Glassware: **Champagne Flute**
Garnish: **Lemon Twist**

- **.75 oz Aperol**
- **.75 oz Luxardo amaretto**
- **.75 oz lemon juice**
- **3 oz prosecco**

1. Combine ingredients in a shaker with ice and shake vigorously.

2. Strain into a champagne flute.

3. Top with Prosecco and garnish with a lemon twist.

— LITTLE RYE LIES —

Whiskey Cake
3601 Dallas Pkwy
Plano, TX 75093
(972) 993-2253
whiskey-cake.com

Whiskey Cake is singlehandedly changing the suburban cocktail landscape in Texas. With locations outside of Dallas, Houston, and San Antonio, they not only serve classic cocktails with the precision of their urban counterparts, but they also host classes and happy hours specifically to educate their guests.

Glassware: **Rocks Glass**
Garnish: **Mint, Orange Peel**

- 2 oz Old Overholt rye whiskey
- .5 oz black tea infused simple syrup
- 2 dashes Reagan's orange bitters
- 1 dash of Angostura bitters

1. Stir all ingredients with rocks ice and strain over a large rock.

2. Garnish with fresh mint and orange peel.

★ ★

"I THINK TEXANS HAVE MORE FUN THAN THE REST OF THE WORLD."

— Tommy June

It's not just the cocktail conference that makes San Antonio one of the most exciting cocktail scenes in the United States, but it certainly helps. Once a year, San Antonio gets to show off to all of those attending the largest cocktail event in Texas. But San Antonio's cocktail history was sparked by the conference's founder, Sasha Petraske.

Sasha became part of the San Antonio community and his training methods and approach changed the culinary scene in San Antonio forever. There are those who do not come directly from Sasha's tutelage, but every single cocktail bar that has opened in San Antonio has benefited by Sasha's presence. Combine world-class training and pedigree with the enormous impact of Mexican culture on the city as a whole, and San Antonio has a different vibe than anywhere in the world.

★ ★

Blue Box
312 Pearl Pkwy #2107
San Antonio, TX 78215
(210) 227-2583
blueboxbar.com

Blue Box Bar is located in the historic Pearl district in San Antonio. Back in the day when the brewery was up and running, employees were allowed to drink on the job. During the day, employees would pull beer from the line to consume, but it was always monitored by the foreman. So the overnight workers, in order to make sure they had the same drinking privileges as their daytime counterparts, kept their beer in an unmarked blue cooler, or the "Blue Box." The Pearl Brewery is no longer operational, but the area has become a haven for incredible food and drinks.

Glassware: **Rocks Glass**

- 4 orange wedges
- 2 dashes cardamon bitters
- .75 oz TX honey syrup 1:1 water honey (TX wildflower honey)
- .75 oz amaro Montenegro
- 1 oz mezcal vida

1. Muddle oranges.

2. Add remaining ingredients plus ice and shake vigorously.

3. Strain into a rocks glass.

Bohanon's
219 E Houston St
San Antonio, TX 78205
(210) 472-2600
bohanans.com

Bohanan's has one of the most important cocktail programs in Texas. By hiring Sasha Petraske (Milk & Honey, The Varnish) they started the cocktail scene in San Antonio. Sasha was hired to revamp the Bohanan's cocktail program in 2010 Texas cocktails have never been the same. With a vision built around education and apprenticeship, the amount of scene-changing bartenders who have come out Bohanan's (and then gone on to train their own crews) is absolutely staggering. If there was a Mount Rushmore of Texas Cocktails, Sasha Petraske would be on it. He's an honorary Texan.

Glassware: **Rocks Glass**
Garnish: **Orange Zest**

- ◆ **2 oz Gentleman Jack**
- ◆ **.25 oz Benedictine**
- ◆ **.75 oz Tempus Fugit Gran Classico**

1. Stir all ingredients and serve over a large rock.

2. Zest an orange as garnish.

—A CONVERSATION WITH —
Jeret Pena

When did cocktails start making sense to you?

I didn't really understand cocktails until I went to go see Bobby Heugel at the Anvil. Three weeks after he opened I went to go see Bobby, and I started watching him make cocktails.

Then Sasha came along. I was working at the bar that all these guys would come drink at after their shifts learning from Sasha. That dove-tailed beautifully because, while I was learning all of these interesting, cool new style[s] of cocktails, I started learning the craft of making traditional, classic cocktails and the technique behind it. It was really interesting, the timing. I was learning technique through Timmy Bryand and Chris Ware.

Then from there, David Allen, my buddy, started talking to Chris Hill, who owns the Esquire Tavern and introduced us and on December 26th in 2010. He offered me the job to run Esquire, the bar program.

Let's chat about the James Beard Award.

Okay… so this starts with Jason Dady telling me that starchefs.com was coming. I looked them up and I realized that, "Oh, no Bobby is in here, Eric Castro is in here. Jason Litrell." So I called Bobby, and asked him what to expect.

And he was like, "Hey, just give them the four best drinks that represents who you are." So, for months, I was just kind of just

wracking my brain like, "What am I going to serve the people?" It turns out I served them four really good drinks.

So cocktail conference comes around and I got a call telling me I won the starchef for the rising star. I put it on mute and was screaming at the top of my lungs.

I usually turn off my ringer, but I got a call at 8:00 in the morning, the day of the gala. My friend, Jennifer McInnis told me I got a James Beard nomination. I was hungover and dehydrated, and emotional. I started crying. I was like, "This is hilarious."

So what does the scene look like now?

Looking at the industry as a whole, I've come to realize that we won, the cocktail movement won. That it's no longer a fad because everyone is doing it. You have places on the Riverwalk that are serving Moscow Mules versus five years ago when that wasn't a thing. Now, we are just a victim of our own success. Now, everyone is doing it, like it's almost kind of lost its allure somewhat.

You can't just be a cocktail bar anymore. I personally think Stay Golden is a good start concept to get—It's a test market. We are testing the market right now. We're creating basically dive craft cocktail bars.

~ THE ONLY WORD ~

Brooklynite
516 Brooklyn Ave
San Antonio, TX 78215
(210) 444-0707
thebrooklynitesa.com

Jeret Pena's first entry into bar ownership is also one of the pivotal bars in San Antonio. Known for its unique use of ingredients and hospitality, The Brooklynite opened in 2012 and was one of the first bars in San Antonio to focus on just cocktails. Coming from the incredible training of the Esquire Tavern, the Brooklynite crew has helped propel San Antonio into one of the most important cocktail scenes in the United States. Jeret's riff on the Last Word makes me strongly consider skipping the gin next time I want one. The citrus still hits you first, but the tequila adds a slightly earthy prickliness that make this cocktail rock.

Glassware: **Coupe Glass**
Garnish: **Lime Wheel**

- .75 oz tequila
- .75 oz lime juice
- .75 oz green chartreuse
- .75 oz maraschino liqueur
- .25 oz mezcal
- Celery bitters

1. Combine ingredients in a shaker with ice and shake vigorously.

2. Strain into a coupe glass.

3. Garnish with a lime.

—Ranger Creek—

TJ, Dennis, and Mark met coming out of business school while working for the same San Antonio corporation. They quickly realized that they were three guys with a passion for beer, whiskey, entrepreneurship, and, most importantly, a growing discontent for corporate life. They literally couldn't decide if they were leaning more towards a brewery or a distillery, so they made both. I mean, how hard could opening up a distillery be? (It's hard. It's incredibly hard. I dare say, kids, don't try this at home…)

Ranger Creek is a combined brewery/distillery located in San Antonio. As a combined operation, they can do things to highlight the relationship between beer and whiskey that not many others can. So much of the equipment is the same to make both beer and whiskey, and there are a lot of similarities between the two processes. They can age their own beer in their own bourbon barrels and distill their beers into whiskeys.

One of the coolest programs they have is their white dog barrel experiment they've been working on for seven years. I've heard of distillers working with small barrels… I've heard of distillers loving them, hating them, and everything in between, but I've never heard of anyone giving the public the opportunity the chance to try the experiment themselves.

Here's how it works, they take their white dog whiskey and they age it in nontraditional small barrels (5 gallons and 10 gallons) and get mature whiskey in about a year. Simultaneously, they age the same white dog whiskey in traditional large barrels (which obviously takes longer) and then do a tasting where you can try the same exact white dog in small and large barrels and do a direct comparison. Mark McDavid, one of the founders of Ranger Creek, said, "No one's ever actually released the results of these experiments, it's just been distillers tasting them behind closed doors. We wanted to present it to the public to try them blind and side by side and they can see what they like better. You have to be kind of nerdy to appreciate it, haha!"

Sidenote: Ranger Creek is also a kickstarter success story. They used the crowdfunding platform to fund their inaugural release of their OPA six packs on the brewery side.

Ranger Creek
Recipe: Dani Call

Nothing like a Texas sweet tea... it can only be improved with some great Texas whiskey.

Glassware: **Rocks Glass**
Garnish: **Orange and Lemon Slices**

- 2 oz sweet tea
- .75 oz pomegranate juice
- 1.5 oz Ranger Creek .36 Texas bourbon
- 1 slice lemon
- 1 slice orange

1. Fill a rocks glass with ice, add ingredients, and stir.

2. Mix liquids in and stir.

3. Rim glass with lemon. Garnish with orange and lemon slices.

Hint: Scale the recipe up to pitcher-size by multiplying all the liquid quantities by 5.

~ BURNING IN EFFIGY ~

Recipe: Benjamin Krick

The Burning in Effigy is a slightly spicy but incredibly fresh drink that's suitable for anything from an anniversary dinner to relaxing on your patio at home. The key, to me, is the Ancho Reyes, which is an ancho chile liqueur. It has a beautiful, hot but not over powering flavor that adds complexity to every drink it's in. Once you've experienced Ancho Reyes, you'll never want to muddle another jalapeno. Just know that a dab will do you. It's a beast.

Glassware: **Coupe Glass**
Garnish: **Abuelita Hot Chocolate, Lemon Peel**

- **2 oz blanco tequila**
- **.5 oz Strega**
- **.5 oz lemon juice**
- **.25 oz Ancho Reyes**
- **.25 oz creme de cacao**

1. Shake all ingredients and double strain into a coupe glass.

2. Served up garnished with a lemon peel and grated abuelita hot chocolate.

—Juniper Tar—

244 W HOUSTON ST
SAN ANTONIO, TX 78205
(210) 229-1833
JUNIPER-TAR.COM

Juniper Tar is incredibly special. It's stylish. It's hip. And most importantly, it's delicious. Benjamin Krick is now the driving force behind the bar and his flair and hospitality shine through every experience at Juniper Tar. While there try the Pamplona, an incredible combination of brandy, two different sherries, and a Kalimoxto reduction.

— DISTRITO FEDERAL —

El Mirador
Recipe: Houston Eaves, El Mirador, 2016
722 S St Mary's St
San Antonio, TX 78205
(210) 225-9444
elmiradorrestaurant.com

San Antonio has had a spicy love affair with El Mirador since Julian and Maria Treviño opened the doors in 1960. Chris Hill, owner of the Esquire Tavern, continued his dedication to preserving San Antonio's culinary history and bought the location in 2014 with the intention to maintain the same sentiments that had been there from the beginning. The greatest addition was the redux of the bar program, Houston Eaves that enhanced the old menu while keeping El Mirador classics like the Margarita Suprema and Leo's Paloma. They have one of the best selections of mezcal anywhere in the state. ¡Salud!

Glassware: **Rocks Glass**
Garnish: **Grapefruit Twist**

- **2 oz Arette Añejo tequila**
- **.75 oz Cocchi di Torino vermouth**
- **1 barspoon Wahaka Espadín mezcal**
- **2 dash Bittermen's Xocolatl mole bitters**
- **1 dash Angostura bitters**

1. Stir very well with ice in a mixing glass, and strain over a large piece of ice in a rocks glass.

2. Express the oil from a wide swath of grapefruit peel over the drink, and garnish with a grapefruit twist.

~ LA TIERRA DE VIEJITAS ~

Recipe: Houston Eaves, Myles Worrell, & Hank Cathey, Downstairs, 2016

I'm frankly thrilled to present La Tierra De Viejitas, namely because I've wanted this recipe from the moment I saw it in a menu.

Glassware: **Beer Glass**
Garnish: **Nutmeg**

- 1.5 oz Lustau Brandy de Jerez Solera Gran Reserva
- .75 oz Café du Monde Chicory Cold Brew
- .5 oz Cardamaro
- 1 oz Henriques & Henriques Rainwater Madeira-Coconut Cream

1. Add madeira-coconut cream to bottom of chilled, tulip-shaped beer glass, and add crushed ice to fill glass.

2. Combine other ingredients in mixing tin, and then pour on top of cream and crushed ice.

3. Garnish with freshly grated nutmeg.

—Esquire Tavern—

155 E COMMERCE ST
SAN ANTONIO, TX 78205
(210) 222-2521
ESQUIRETAVERN-SA.COM

The Esquire Tavern is San Antonio history. The door originally opened on Repeal Day in 1933. San Antonio's oldest bar went through a massive makeover in 2011. Its vintage décor, classic furnishings, and dusky lighting which creates an intimate, yet lively atmosphere. This is the only Riverwalk bar you need to go to in San Antonio, trust me.

There's one in every city... one bar that is quintessentially the centerpiece of their entire scene. The Esquire Tavern is that for San Antonio. Maybe it's the James Beard nominations for best bar program (they have two) or maybe it's the pedigree of those who have been a part of the program and moved on to other amazing projects, but it's certainly one of the most respected and revered bars in all of Texas. Houston Eaves is now leading the bar program, and you can see his agave centric roots all over the menu.

⌁ ¡SIN MAÍZ NO HAY PAÍS! ⌁

Esquire Tavern Downstairs
Recipe: Houston Eaves, Myles Worrell, & Hank Cathey, Downstairs, 2016
155 E Commerce St
San Antonio, TX 78205
(210) 222-2521

esquiretavern-sa.com/downstairs

Okay, so... here's a little secret... there's a speakeasy inside a cocktail bar in San Antonio. Meta, I know. But the Downstairs at Esquire Tavern is truly a different world than the raucous party happening above. With Hank Cathey coming up with some of the most innovative drinks and drink presentations in the city, Downstairs is an experience in and of its own. With an entrance on the Riverwalk itself, Downstairs is an intimate lounge dishing out "unconventional inclinations." This place is nice. I'm talking really nice. This isn't a cocktail dive bar... this is, unapologetically, the nicest bar on the Riverwalk and the drinks are absolutely incredible. This big batch recipe will make you look like a rockstar party host.

Glassware: **Rocks Glass**
Garnish: **Mint Sprig, Nutmeg**

- **4 qts Jamaican rum (Hamilton Jamaican gold)**
- **1 qt lime juice**
- **3 qts pineapple juice**
- **2 qts orange juice**

- **1 qt sherry (1:1:1 Fino:Oloroso:Palo Cortado)**
- **4 qts whole milk**
- **16 oz coconut cream**
- **32 oz corn**

258 — TEXAS COCKTAILS

1. Combine rum, lime juice, pineapple juice, orange juice, and sherry to create a juice mix.

2. In a large pot, combine whole milk, coconut cream, and corn. Heat until boiling. Strain corn. Slowly add liquid to juice mix.

3. Strain through a super bag slowly. Continue to strain mixture no less than three times, changing out the catch container but not the super bag, after each strain has run through.

4. The more you strain, the more clear the punch will be. Each passing through will take longer than the last. Do not agitate the bag in any way while straining.

5. Bottle and chill.

6. Serve individually over large piece of ice in a rocks glass, and garnish with mint sprig and grated nutmeg. Enjoy!

—A CONVERSATION WITH—
Cathy Siegel

When did the San Antonio Cocktail Conference begin?

Well, the first cocktail conference was held in January of 2012.

Were you there?

Yes, when I participated the first year, that was because I was the Executive Director of the original beneficiary agency from the cocktail conference.

So, how was it? What was it like?

A bunch of people who are all friends joined hands and jumped off the edge of the cliff and they never looked down to see if there was water. They were just confident that if they held hands and they were all friends and they believed in each other and they believed in the cause that everything would be fine. It was. They didn't have some great master plan and the blueprints for a successful event. They just believed in the cause and in each other.

What was the cause?

The original beneficiary agency. We were giving money to help bring children to San Antonio from all over the world, from developing countries, who needed our help to get repaired with heart surgery. It felt good to be doing it for charity, and to be doing good in Texas. From the beginning, participating industry people from out of town would say it felt like doing a festival in your neighborhood.

Even as we've grown, I think we maintained that feeling with people. We issued almost 10,000 tickets in 2017. We have people coming from all over the world and yet it still feels like a neighbor-

I think it feels really good to the food and beverage community to do this event together to benefit children's causes. And it feels really good to show off our city and our talents this way.

I would tell you that the growth of the cocktail scene in San Antonio, if you look at the number of true craft cocktail bars in the city in 2011 until now, the growth of the number of places and the growth of the cocktail conference, my guess would be similar.

Same question but for Texas.

I think it's the exact same thing. I think its growth matches our own growth. I think it felt good to bring this to people down to Texas. Texans are a funny breed and we are very, very vocal about our pride in being from or living in Texas.

In Texas we are Texans. I am proud of people coming to San Antonio to experience the San Antonio cocktail conference. I think we as Texans are proud that this massive amount of people are coming to Texas to celebrate craft cocktails.

What are other differentiators between SACC and other cocktail events across the country?

First and foremost, the charity component. That ... 100% of our profits go to support children's charities. That makes it different right off the bat. Also we have much more involvement from the consumer in our festival than in any other festival I can think of. We are creating more competent consumers. That's really wonderful.

What's on the docket for the future of SACC?

I hope that the future of SACC is such that more and more people will want to invest their time, energy, and dollars in the product so that we can begin to grow our contribution to children's care. I hope that we will continue to reach more and more people throughout the United States so that we can continue to grow this community of people that enjoy craft cocktails together. We intend to be around for a long time, but as we grow what I hope is that we are always approachable.

— KAMEHAMEHA —

Hot Joy
1014 S Alamo St
San Antonio, TX 78210
(210) 368-9324
hotjoysa.com

First and foremost, I've been trying to avoid talking about anything that's not cocktail related, but I have to divert for a second. IF you ever find yourself in San Antonio and you are in desperate need for ramen... Go. To. Hot. Joy. There's a reason it was on Bon Appetit's Top 10 list the year it opened. You'll thank me for this. Hot Joy's always had a killer cocktail program with some of San Antonio's top talent passing through. The Kamehameha is named after the founder and first ruler of Hawaii. It also happens to be a signature move of Goku, the hero of Dragonball Z. So, you see, it has Japanese whisky blended with American whiskey. Get it?

Glassware: **Rocks Glass**
Garnish: **Lemon Twist**

- 1 oz Suntory Toki Japanese whisky
- .5 oz Takara Shochu
- .5 oz Rittenhouse rye
- .5 oz Punt e Mes
- 2 dashes Angostura bitters

1. Add all ingredients to a rocks glass with one large ice cube.

2. Garnish with a lemon twist and a smile.

THE RATTLE AND THE RHYTHM

Jazz, TX
Recipe: Jake Corney
312 Pearl Parkway, Bld. #6 Suite #6001
San Antonio, TX 78215
(210) 332-9386
jazztx.com

Jazz, TX is a 3,500-square-foot live music venue in a basement in the Pearl District in San Antonio. A Sasha Petraske disciple Jake Corney (formerly at Bohanan's) has crafted a magnificent menu based on the live music vibes ranging from jazz to honky tonk to blues. It's one of the more approachable, yet creative menus in San Antonio, and this cocktail is incredibly refreshing and dangerously easy to drink.

Glassware: **Rocks Glass**
Garnish: **Mint**

- • **1.5 oz white rum**
- • **.75 oz lime juice**
- • **.75 oz simple syrup**
- • **.75 oz Jicama Juice**

- • **3–4 mint leaves**
- • **1 pinch smoked sea salt**
- • **2 dashes coffee bitters**

1. Shake all ingredients and strain into a rocks glass.

2. Garnish with mint to serve.

⌐ THE MISSIONARY ⌐

Last Word
229 E Houston St #10
San Antonio, TX 78205
(210) 314-1285

thelastwordsa.com

Hidden under Houston Street in downtown San Antonio, Last Word is a Jeret Pena joint. Stellar service, super cool vibe, and you just feel fancy when you're walking down those stairs. The Missionary again utilizes Texas grapefruits and the gin selection and this one, for me, is key. I'd try it with a Highborn if you're aiming for a Texas gin, otherwise, Ford's gin is always delicious.

Glassware: **Rocks Glass**
Garnish: **Grapefruit Peel**

- ⋄ **1.5 oz gin**
- ⋄ **1 oz mixed berry shrub**
- ⋄ **.75 oz grapefruit juice**
- ⋄ **2 cucumbers**

1. Shake all ingredients and strain into a rocks glass.

2. Top with ice and a grapefruit peel.

EGG WHITE FOAM

- In a bowl (copper is preferred)
- 2½–3 oz egg whites.
- 3 Dashes of black walnut bitters
- Splash of Cherry Heering

Whip until firm.

THE FRIENDLY STRANGER ⁓
IN THE BLACK SEDAN

Soho
Recipe: Lufty Flores Vico
214 W Crockett St
San Antonio, TX 78205
(210) 444-1000

And now we talk about a San Antonio OG, Lutfy Flores Vico. Since 2008, SoHo Wine and Martini Bar has served some pretty out-there concoctions. This also became one of the spots where the fellas being trained by Sasha Petraske down the street would hang after their shifts. Lutfy's been there from the humble beginnings of cocktails in San Antonio, no matter how you slice it. The best part is that Soho feels like the type of place an OG would call home.

Glassware: **Coupe Glass**
Garnish: **Black Walnut Bitters, Cherry Heering, Egg White Foam**

- 2.5 oz Old Forester Statesman
- .5 oz Grand Marnier
- .5 oz Cherry Heering
- Splash of water

1. Add all ingredients to a mixing glass. Add ice and stir.

2. Pour into a chilled coupe glass.

3. Top with bitters, cherry, and foam. Spray orange oils over foam and serve.

—Azar Distilling—

At about 8:15 AM on October 24th, 2014, there was an explosion at Azar Distilling, strong enough to send a man flying through (yes—through) a wall. A small fire was started and it took Bexar County firefighters about 40 minutes to put out the flames. The worker was sent to the hospital, but sustained no injuries... but now he has a hell of a story.

When he arrived on the scene, Trey Azar feared he'd lost everything. To lighten the mood, the volunteer firefighters suggested that he rename the brand "Cinco Fuego." Through sheer force of will, they re-opened just 95 days after the blast.

Proudly hailing from San Antonio, Trey and Kimberly Azar started Azar Distilling in 2010 named after (kinda) their five children. Trey's family has always been in the booze business. His grandfather was the first ever distributor of Coors in Texas, but his family sold off their chain of liquor stores some time ago. The oil and gas industry just wasn't cutting it for him, so Trey and wife Kim decided to jump back on the wagon by designing a premium American vodka, which has won multiple awards in international competitions.

Fast forward to today and here comes Seersucker Gin. Trey said, "We worked for more than a year to accomplish the perfect taste profile that is light on the palate and has recognizable Southern flavors, yet still maintains the nuances that a gin drinker appreciates." Utilizing the same pot distillation as Cinco Vodka, Seersucker is a slick designed, citrus forward gin with notes of honeysuckle and mint to compliment the juniper.

Azar Distilling is in the process of expanding, not just the scope of the brands, but the distillery itself. Cinco Vodka and Seersucker Gin are now available at most major liquor stores throughout Texas, Tennessee, Arkansas, Massachusetts, Oklahoma, and Rhode Island.

⌐ SEERSUCKER 75 ⌐

Azar Distilling
8501 Cover Rd
San Antonio, TX 78263
(210) 648-1500
cincovodka.com

This is a French 75, made with Seersucker gin. This is a recipe you should commit to memory.

Glassware: **Champagne Glass**
Garnish: **Lemon Twist**

- • **1 oz Seersucker gin**
- • **.5 oz lemon juice**
- • **.5 oz simple syrup**
- • **Prosecco or champagne**

1. Combine ingredients in a shaker with ice and shake vigorously.

2. Strain into a champagne glass.

3. Top with chilled prosecco or champagne.

4. Garnish with a lemon twist.

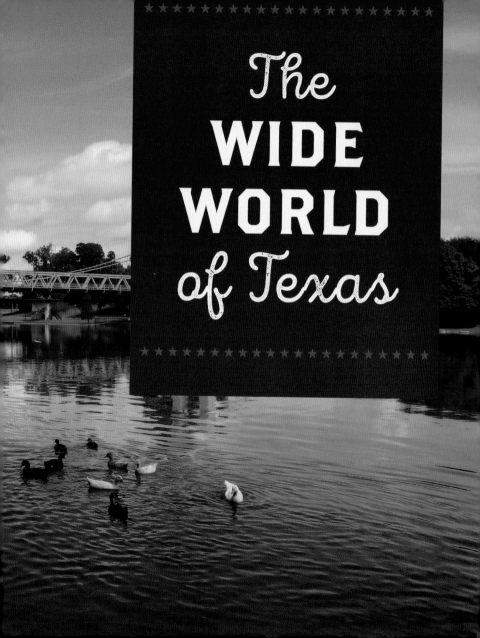

★ ★

"TEXAS IS NEITHER SOUTHERN NOR WESTERN.
TEXAS IS TEXAS."

—Senator William Blakley

The population of Marfa is 1981, and I have a recipe for you from there. The population of Boerne is 10,471 and I have a recipe for you from there. The population of Texarkana is 34,782 and I have a recipe for you from there.

I think you get the point. When I started this project, I kept picturing a map of Texas. The first thing I said to myself was "You can't just have Dallas, Austin, Houston, and San Antonio." I went into this blindly hoping that the cocktail movement had made it to the hinterlands. Y'all... it has. From McAllen to Amarillo and El Paso to Texarkana, the map's filling itself out nicely. The fact that Waco has gone, in my mind, from that place where they won't let you dance (listen, there were lots of rumors about the Baptists running Baylor) to one of the most important whiskey cities in the world, let alone Texas, is no small feat itself.

Texas is massive. This chapter is the reason I wanted to present this book in this manner. Cocktails are everywhere and I have the map to prove it. While this movement may have started in the city centers, it's the suburbs and the college towns that are coming in to their own. If you can have a cocktail bar, in the shadow of Kyle Field, be one of the most happening spots in College Station, the world's changed, y'all.

★ ★

ROSEMARY SIMPLE
SYRUP

- 1 cup water
- 8 oz by weight sugar

⟿ SMOKEY THE PEAR ⟿

Black Pearl
108 W Erwin St
Tyler, TX 75702
(903) 531-2415

It takes some courage to throw cocktails on a menu in Tyler, Texas, but if you're going to do it, you might as well be exceptional at it. Lead by Mitch Murray, Black Pearl serves stellar original and classic cocktails. Their cocktail is based on an unfortunately underused Texas product, the mighty pear. Texas pears are pretty amazing and, often, more available than one might think. In fact, every now and then you'll see pears on abandoned farm sites that are over 100 years old. This is a great combination of the freshness of the pears and the smoke from the rosemary with an underbelly of some magnificent TX whiskey.

Glassware: **Rocks Glass**
Garnish: **Rosemary Sprig**

- **2 oz TX Blended Whiskey**
- **.75 oz Grand Marnier**
- **1 oz lemon juice**
- **.5 oz rosemary simple syrup**
- **¼ of a pear**

1. Add pear, lemon juice, and simple syrup to shaker tin.

2. Muddle the pear, and add remaining ingredients.

3. Shake and fine strain into a rosemary-smoked rocks glass over a large ice cube.

4. Garnish with a fresh rosemary sprig.

~ RUMBLE OF THE GODS ~

Dichotomy Coffee & Spirits
508 Austin Ave
Waco, TX 76701
dichotomycs.com

If I was to have you guess what the whiskey capital of Texas was, how many of you would have said Waco? Balcones is one of the most important whiskey producers in the United States, let alone Texas. Rumble is a particularly interesting spirit. Originally built on a dessert sauce template, Rumble isn't a whiskey, nor is it a mead... is it an eau de vie? Maybe? Regardless, it's become a Texas staple and that's why you'll see it all over Dichotomy's menu in Waco, Texas. Dichotomy is half cocktail bar, half coffee shop and they've brought true cocktail culture to Waco, which is quite impressive.

Glassware: Nick & Nora
Garnish: Orange Rind, Maraschino Cherry

- 1.5 oz rumble
- .75 oz orange liqueur
- .75 oz lime juice
- .25 oz simple syrup

1. Shake all ingredients and double strain into glass.

2. Garnish with orange rind and maraschino cherry.

—Balcones Distilling—

We're blessed here in the great state of Texas with some incredible terroir, an incredible climate, and some damn creative Texans. Balcones makes some of the best whiskey on the planet. Not state, not country, but planet. What started off as the mad scientist Chip Tate and his merry gang of innovators, Balcones has continued to turn out some unbelievable products since 2008.

Chip Tate is no longer at Balcones. When I swung by his new project and casually said that I was heading to Balcones after, he said, "well don't tell them you were here. I'm he who shall not be named." The break up wasn't the easiest, but I'm not going to get in to that... mostly because everyone told me far too much information and that saga is a book in and of itself. Break ups happen... who knows? Maybe we'll just end up with two world-class whiskey distilleries in Waco. That's what I'd like to think anyway.

Balcones 2.0 is doing just fine. They have always meticulously sought out ingredients for their richness in flavor. From blue corn grown in New Mexico to the first Texas-grown malted barley, every spirit they make aims for being recognizable and delectable. This translates to a delightful weight on the tongue, giving their whiskey a distinct density on the palate.

In 2011, they purchased the Texas Fireproof Storage Co. building in downtown Waco. Built in 1923, it is a massive structure of concrete, steel, and brick, and has 65,000 square feet of space (about 25 times larger than the first distillery). At the end of 2016, Balcones 2.0 officially opened their doors to the public and it's turned in to a great place to watch distilling happen. Balcones has made a significant investment not only in their operation, but also in their community of Waco.

I asked Jared Himstedt, Balcones head distiller, who freely admitted that he's not a cocktail guy, what cocktails he's seen with Balcones that have caught his eye. "There's always been some top-end mixologists that have done cool things with the Rumble... otherwise I love it when I see replacing tequila or mezcal with Brimstone. It's surprisingly cool." He took the words right out of my mouth. Balcones is available pretty much nationwide at your local enormous liquor store.

— THE PEACEFUL PEOPLE —

Balcones Distilling
Recipe: Maria Vieira from The East London Liquor Company
in London, UK
225 S 11th St
Waco, TX 76701
(254) 755-6003
balconesdistilling.com

This one's fun. Balcones makes incredibly mixable spirits, and while they're brilliant alone, when given to a great bartender, they add complexities that can't be replicated.

Glassware: Clay Cups
Garnish: None

- 1.5 oz Balcones Baby Blue
- 1 teaspoon/barspoon mezcal
- .75 oz toasted butter pecan

syrup
- .5 oz lemon juice
- 3 dashes of coffee bitters

1. Combine all ingredients and shake with ice.

2. Strain into traditional clay cups.

3. Serve with a side of blue corn bread with extra butter pecan syrup for dipping!

Toasted Butter Pecan Syrup

- 100 gr pecan halves
- 300 gr/ml water
- 260 g caster sugar
- 10 ml melted butter
- 2 g xantham gum, optional

1. Moisturize the pecans in a solution of baking soda, water, and a pinch of sugar for 10 minutes.

2. Dry the pecans with a cloth and then toast them in the oven.

3. Crush the pecans and soak them in water to extract the oils and make a milk.

4. After 2 hours, blend the milk and pecans in a food processor.

5. Fine strain the liquid in a cheese cloth, gently squeezing by hand. You should have about 260 gr of toasted pecan milk at this point.

6. Add equal part of caster sugar (260 gr in this case) and mix it well until dissolved.

7. Add 10 ml of melted butter.

8. Add 2 gr of xantham gum.

~ THE BITTER POMELO ~

Cochineal
107 W San Antonio St
Marfa, TX 79843
(432) 729-3300
cochinealmarfa.com

Cochineal has been the go-to hot spot in Marfa for years. With Alexandra Gates taking over ownership in 2017, the tradition of frequent menu changes and seasonal offers carries on. Sabine said, "Alexandra and I are both European and grew up drinking Campari Orange or Aperol and have a love for bitter drinks and aperitifs. Because the restaurant also has a large garden where we grow lots of our own vegetables and all of our herbs, so we incorporate garden herbs in lots of drinks. So, we'd like to re-introduce our customers to the lost art of before-dinner drinks if you will, plus they stimulate and cleanse the palate."

Glassware: **Highball Glass**
Garnish: **Mint Sprig**

- 2 oz Cynar
- 4 oz fresh Texas ruby red grapefruit juice

- 3 to 5 mint leaves, crushed

1. Mix all ingredients and stir until incorporated.

2. Strain into a highball and top off with Topo Chico.

3. Garnish with a sprig of mint.

— HIBISCUS MARGARITA —

Mexican Sugar
7501 Lone Star Dr B150
Plano, TX 75024
(972) 943-0984
mexicansugarcocina.com

I am, unashamedly, a draft cocktail nerd. If you've read this sucker cover to cover, you know why. The use of draft cocktails at Mexican Sugar is one of the coolest innovations in craft service that I've seen in a very long time. They have almost 20 draft cocktails on the menu! Coming from the folks behind Whiskey Cake and Ida Claire, Mexican Sugar is another entry into the suburban cocktail arena. The bar program is a tribute to all cocktails latin, utilizing ingredients like chica morada (Peruvian purple corn) or jicama juice or the inclusion of one of their massive collection of agave spirits. Also, this is a simple, tasty upgrade to your margarita.

Glassware: **Coupe Glass**
Garnish: **Lime Wheel**

- 1.75 oz reposado tequila
- .5 oz orange liqueur
- .75 oz hibiscus water
- .5 oz simple syrup
- .5 oz fresh lime juice
- Barspoon velvet falernum

1. Combine ingredients in a shaker with ice and shake vigorously.

2. Fine strain into a chilled coupe glass.

3. Garnish with a lime wheel.

~ BOURBON COBBLER ~

Metropolitan
9181 Town Square Blvd Suite 1201
Amarillo, TX 79119
(806) 242-0117
metroofamarillo.com

Metropolitan is in Amarillo. You read that correctly. Amarillo. Cocktail culture has come to the panhandle, my friends. Playing off of historical speakeasies, there are some pretty humorous house rules that must be obeyed. "Don't bring anyone that you wouldn't bring to your mom's house on Sunday" is probably the one that we all should try to live by a little more often, but I digress. The color of this bourbon cobbler reminds me of an Amarillo sunset and is best consumed while watching one.

Glassware: **Wine Goblet**
Garnish: **Lemon Twist**

- **1.66 oz Eagle Rare bourbon**
- **.66 oz Luxardo Liquer**
- **.5 oz simple syrup**
- **3 peels each of lemon, orange, and grapefruit**

Stir all ingredients. Add a little ice and pour into a rocks-filled wine goblet.

—Dripping Springs—

"Are you from Texas originally?" Kevin Kelleher, founder of San Luis Spirits asked me.

"I am, sir, born and raised."

"Okay, then you'll get it then…"

San Luis Spirits, who makes Dripping Springs Vodka, was the second distiller in Texas.

Founded by brothers Gary and Kevin Kelleher, the company's first distribution was in April 2007. They're located in Dripping Springs, Texas, gateway to the Texas Hill Country.

"In 2006, it was a little more difficult than it would be (starting a distillery) today. It took 16 months, and until you have your license, you're not supposed to be doing anything, so you just did a bunch of planning and hoped it went through," Kevin told me.

"We started at a good time. We wound up sort of being the Pepsi to Tito's Coke. I will say that 10 years ago the acceptance of a Texas liquor brand didn't exist and didn't resonate with people. I wouldn't say it came naturally… but if you fast forward to today… because of Tito's, because of Deep Eddy, because of ourselves, because of Balcones, because of Garrison, because of some higher quality products, it turned into a way to a branding concept. It definitely is accepted as a place that makes great spirits, compared to what it used to be."

Then Kelleher's great aunt, who was originally from Russia (she was sent to Siberia by Catherine the Great for being German) used to tell them stories about how her grandfather was rumored to have made vodka for the Czar. Dripping Springs makes some of the most original vodka in Texas, made with artesian spring water and a Swedish activated charcoal filtration. It's balanced, with a smooth finish. They are distributed nationwide.

~ WATERMELON DAYS ~

Dripping Springs
5330 Bell Springs Rd
Dripping Springs, TX 78620
(512) 858-1199
drippingspringsvodka.com

This is a simple way to spice up a summer cocktail. You should make a big batch and head out to float the river.

Glassware: Mason Jar
Garnish: Watermelon Slice

- **2 oz Dripping Springs vodka**
- **Fresh watermelon pieces, chopped fine**
- **1 slice fresh jalapeño**
- **½ lime, juiced**

1. Place all ingredients into a shaker filled with ice.

2. Shake vigorously, pour into a mason jar, and garnish with a slice of watermelon.

Peggy's on the Green
128 W Blanco Rd
Boerne, TX 78006
(830) 572-5000

peggysonthegreen.com

Peggy's on the Green is named for the late mother of Chef/ Owner Mark Bohanan, who was a great cook in her own right. Located in the historic Kendall Inn, an old stagecoach stop, Peggy's on the Green is from the founders of Bohanan's and the San Antonio Cocktail Conference. It's cocktails and elevated comfort food in the Hill County... I mean come on y'all... this is basically a Texan utopia.

Glassware: **Collins Glass**
Garnish: **Orange Zest**

- **1.5 oz bourbon**
- **.5 oz Cynar**
- **.5 oz Punt e Mes**
- **.5 oz lemon juice**
- **.25 oz simple syrup**
- **2-4 dashes Angostura bitters**
- **Top with soda**

Shake all ingredients. Double strain into collins glass filled with ice. Top with soda. Twist zest over drink and drop in.

—Tate & Company—

There aren't too many people in the world that have created such a following that they deserved to be talked about without an operable distillery. To peel back the curtain a bit… as I write this, it's "fall." The book, I've been told, comes out in "the spring." Tate & Company Distillery should be open by the time you read this. Or not. But regardless, if they're open, they're making some of the best products in the state. How do I know? It's Chip F-ing Tate.

In 2008, Chip Tate started Balcones. Balcones became one of the most re-knowned, most awarded, most respected craft whiskey distilleries in the country, if not the world. They won 140 awards from 2010 to 2014. Also in August 2014, Tate and his investors found themselves in court. After the resulting legal battle, Chip was out and Balcones continued without his guidance.

Chip is now acknowledged as a leader in the craft distilling industry, having received more than 150 national and international awards, including US Craft Distillery of the Year and Global Distillery of the Year from the Wizards of Whisky International Competition. In recognition of his contributions to the development of the craft spirits industry, *Whisky Magazine* awarded him their inaugural Craft Whiskey Distillery of the Year Icon award in 2012, a category which he won again two years later. In 2013, The Spirits Business named him a Grand Master of World Whisky and in the following year, at the prestigious World Whisky Awards in London, he won the Best Overall American Whisky.

Chip's newest ventures, Tate & Company Distillery and Chip Tate Craft Copperworks, could very well end up being the most exciting chapter yet. Using the skills, expertise, and relationships he has developed to date, Chip is aspiring to make Tate & Company Distillery a haven for the craft movement, while his Tate Craft Copperworks is the world's first, distiller-led manufacturer and designer of artisanal copper pot stills. Together, Tate & Company Distillery and Chip Tate Craft Copperworks are creating and fostering a new environment of creative collaboration for dedicated distillers around the world.

So here's what you have. Some cool pictures, and a promise of greatness… Whatever Tate & Company Distillery is selling, you should go buy.

—A CONVERSATION WITH —
Chip Tate

Alright man, let's start from the beginning...

Yes. Well, let's see, I really fell in love with cooking and fermentation when I was relatively young. Then in college I got into the brewing properly.

What was the first spirit that you made?

First spirits that I made were a honey and fig spirit and a blue corn whiskey. Some of that was strictly creative but some of that was philosophically intentional... With the whiskey, I wanted to make something that went out of its way to not be bourbon, but still something that was interesting to American whiskey drinkers. And the other was kind of the chef turned distiller...

We won't go into the why, but you're no longer at your original distillery. So, how about now? What are you up to now?

Well, we're building a quite remarkable craft distillery. It's going to be about the size of Balvenie, but with the capability to make just

about anything. It'll allow us to do a lot of things that I've come up with but never had the capacity. For instance, I never felt like it would be okay to tinker with the stills when we're promising people bottles they couldn't get of stuff we already sold them.

I'm sure they appreciated that. Are you incorporating anything particularly exciting?

We've got some cool cooperative projects that I can't go into yet that cross state and national borders. We're really trying to just set up a good, strong, long-term craft distillery that we'll be able to look back 20 years from now and say this is a stable thing.

What's been your biggest challenge with the new distillery?

This is hard and expensive and time-consuming and expensive to set up a distillery to actually produce some things measured in millions. We have two 2,500 gallons in a direct fire pot stills with interesting mixing manifolds and infrared burners. We have four double steam jacketed spirit stills. We have a full malt kit small we're about to break ground on a 50,000 square foot rickhouse that I already know is going to be too small.

Did you ever consider leaving Texas?

Hell no, absolutely not. My house is here, all my friends are here, why would I leave? Besides, I need to make sure there's at least one good distillery here.

— Ironroot Distillery—

According to *Whisky Magazine*, which may have some pedigree in these sorts of things, the world's best corn whiskey comes from Ironroot Republic Distillery in Denison. "We love our whiskey," Robert Likarish, co-founder of Ironroot, said. "We think it's great, but for a distillery our age to be as young as we are to win an award like this is completely unheard of."

Ironroot is Texas, through and through… run by Texans, making Texas spirits, using Texas grain. From grain to glass, as they say, Ironroot is one of the most impressive operations in the state. They're creative in all the right ways. Creative use of grains? Yep. Obsession with locality of source materials? Oh yeah. Funky barrel-aging techniques? I had one they finished in both port and Islay barrels… so yes. Good lord, yes.

One of the weirder and cooler things that I learned about at Ironroot was starka. Starka is barrel-aged vodka and has been popular in Eastern Europe since the 15th century. Families would bury barrels of starka when a child was born and then when it was their wedding day, they'd dig it up and party. Ironroot is making Texas starka and it's pretty interesting… It's similar to a whiskey and the spirit certainly pulls flavors out of the wood — vanilla, caramel, chocolate, and fruit, but it's definitely an aged vodka. Give it a try.

This is a family affair. Along with Robert, his brother Jonathan is the co-founder and head distiller, and their mom keeps the boys in line. The biggest outlier here, to me, is the training… these guys initially trained in cognac and then wound up spending a lot of time with Chip Tate down in Waco. They're taking techniques that aren't traditionally used for whiskey and making some of the best corn whiskey on the planet with it. Jonathan said, "How we run the stills is a lot closer to the way that the French run their cognac stills than American whiskey."

This is an exceptional distillery. Their creativity seemingly has no bounds. Of all of the whiskey joints in Texas, this is one to watch.

~ IRONROOT ICED TODDY ~

Ironroot Distillery
100 Church Ave
College Station, TX 77840
(979) 721-9156
westendelixircompany.com

This is a perfect drink for fall, or even if you're under the weather. Whiskey cures all.

Glassware: **Rocks Glass**
Garnish: **Lemon Peel**

- 1 oz Ironroot Harbinger
- 1 oz lemonade
- 1 oz honey simple syrup
- ¼ oz fresh lemon juice

1. Shake all ingredients in a shaker with ice.

2. Pour in rocks glass filled with ice.

3. Garnish with lemon peel.

Honey Simple Syrup:

Heat up ½ cup of water and ½ cup of honey into the water. Stir and then let honey simple syrup cool to room temperature before using.

~ THE OLD WORLD ~

West End Elixir Company
100 Church Ave
College Station, TX 77840
(979) 721-9156

westendelixircompany.com

Cocktails in Aggieland? Whoop! The West End Elixir Company is the first bar of its kind in the Bryan–College Station area. After three tours of duty in the Marine Corps, Dustin Batson moved to Aggieland to attend Texas A&M. He opened West End Elixir Company in 2015 and has been elevating the drinking scene in College Station ever since.

Glassware: **Rocks Glass**
Garnish: **Peach Slice**

- **2 slices muddled peach**
- **1 scoop brown sugar**
- **2 dashes peach bitters**
- **.5 oz St. Germaine Elderflower liqueur**
- **1.5 oz Bulleit Bourbon**

1. Stir all ingredients.

2. Add ice, garnish with a peach slice, and serve.

TURBINADO SYRUP

- 2 parts turbinado sugar
- 1 part hot water

Combine and stir until sugar is
completely dissolved.

⟶ PORTER FLIP ⟵

Preamble Lounge & Craft House
Recipe: Sage Sharp
20801 Gulf Fwy #12
Webster, TX 77598
(832) 905-2927

preamblelounge.com

As of late, beer cocktails have become a great addition to today's on cocktail programs. It's a collection of flavor profiles that you can play with if your bar also has a great beer selection, like so many quality programs today do. At Preamble in Webster, they make a remarkable flip with a coffee porter base. 8th Wonder is a great Houston brewery and if you can get it, their Rocket Fuel porter is perfect in this cocktail. Suburban cocktails man, I'm telling you… these places are the future.

Glassware: **Coupe Glass**
Garnish: **Ground Cinnamon**

- **2 oz 8th Wonder Rocket Fuel Vietnamese coffee porter (flattened)**
- **1.5 oz spiced rum**
- **1 oz turbinado syrup**
- **1 whole egg**

1. Combine all ingredients and dry shake without ice for 10 seconds.

2. Shake with ice for 30 seconds.

3. Fine mesh strain into a coupe glass.

4. Garnish with ground cinnamon.

—Garrison Brothers Distillery—

Garrison Brothers made some of the first whiskey in Texas. In fact, they were the 29th distillery in the United States (now there are over 1500) and they were literally having to explain to regulatory entities how distilling works and what they should be looking for when they come to do an inspection. Dan Garrison, the founder, had approached Tito Beveridge multiple times about starting a distillery. "I know he wanted to make whiskey and I told him I was going to, but [I] think he didn't believe me," laughed Garrison.

In 2004, Dan Garrison walked away from a financially rewarding but volatile career as a software marketing professional. After numerous trips to Kentucky to learn how to make bourbon, Garrison set up shop on his small farm and ranch in the Hill Country. He borrowed money from friends and family. He built a small "experimental barn" and began tinkering with equipment, tanks, pumps, plumbing, steam, barrels, grain, and yeast. In November 2007, he bought an antique pot still named The Copper Cowgirl who was originally built in 1972 for Wild Turkey.

The following year, Garrison uncorked one of the bourbon barrels, tasted the 7 month old bourbon, and immediately began to beg, borrow, and steal to build a bigger distillery. Since then, bottles of Garrison Brothers Texas Straight Bourbon Whiskey has become quite sought after. Five vintages have been released and each has sold out in a matter of days, and when a new release is announced, bourbon drinkers road-trip to the Hill Country to get one.

Garrison is proud of his bourbon. It's expensive and Garrison is quick to defend that. The entire time we were chatting it felt like he was alluding to something. "Honor the spirit." "Why would anyone want to put something in bourbon?" "Cocktails are alright but I drink bourbon." "Once you add something, it's not bourbon." So I asked him...

"Dan. Do you hate cocktails?"

He said, "No, absolutely not. I tend to be a little bit of an antago-
nist, but I am the first person to admit that I know next to nothing
about making a great cocktail. Zero. Zilch. Nada. My standard go-to is
a Garrison Brothers on the rocks with a splash of Topo Chico, served in
a 32-ounce YETI Rambler. I can sip on one of those for days."

Unfortunately for Dan, Garrison Brothers Texas Straight Bourbon
Whiskey makes some damn fine drinks. So we'll include two of them...
the one that Dan recommends and the one that we do.

The Perfect Garrison
- Two parts Garrison Brothers Texas Straight Bourbon Whiskey
- One part glass

~ REV'S HILL COUNTRY DONKEY ~

Garrison Brothers Distilling
Recipe: Jason P. Brand, Garrison Brothers Distillery, Hye, Texas
1827 Hye-Albert Rd
Hye, TX 78635
(830) 392-0246

garrisonbros.com

"**A**fter working an event in Austin one hot-as-hell summer day, I was on my way back to the still house in Hye. Needing a break on this grueling hour-and-a-half drive, I decided to stop by a "hole in the wall" bar for a drink. As I sat down at the bar I noticed a young hipster couple drinking something out of cold, sweaty copper mugs. Now, as a distiller I have a fondness for copper, because copper is shiny, and Rev loves shiny things. I asked what it was, and the bartender told me it was a Moscow Mule, which is made with vodka. Well, frankly, vodka sucks. I once heard a wise man say 'vodka is intended for rich women on diets.' I have to agree. Still, wanting to get a drink from the cold, shiny copper mug and noticing they had our bourbon behind the bar, I asked if he would mind replacing the dietary supplement with Garrison Brothers Texas Straight Bourbon, and add extra lime juice. Rev's Hill Country Donkey was born!"—Reverend Jason Brand, Distillery Director, Garrison Brothers.

Glassware: **Copper Mug**
Garnish: **Lime Wedge**

- **2.5 oz Garrison Brothers Texas Straight bourbon whiskey**
- **Juice from half of lime**
- **Fever Tree or your favorite ginger beer**

1. Fill copper mug with crushed ice.

2. Add ginger beer, bourbon, and lime juice.

3. Lime wedge on rim as garnish.

4. For an extra kick, use spicy ginger beer!

⚊ PITAYA-RITA ⚊

Salt New American Table
Recipe: Daniel Copado
210 N Main St
McAllen, TX 78504
(956) 627-6304

saltnewamericantable.com

Location, location, location. Your cocktails, like your food, should be different, contingent on where you are consuming them. It's a key element in the way Chef Larry Delgado runs Salt in McAllen, but it has brilliantly impacted the bar program as well. The Pitaya-rita is a valley cocktail through and through. It begins with Pitaya Farms dragon fruit from Raymondville, Texas, and Texas Valley lemons from Hernandez Farms in Weslaco, Texas, This is about as local as you can get... but if Pitaya dragon fruit isn't available, whatever you can find will do just fine.

Glassware: **Rocks Glass**
Garnish: **Dragon Fruit Slice**

- **1.5 oz Chefs Select Patron reposado**
- **1 oz dragon fruit puree**
- **1.25 oz Texas Valley lemons**
- **.75 oz agave nectar**
- **.75 oz Gran Marnier**

1. Combine ingredients in a shaker with ice and shake vigorously.

2. Strain into a rocks glass.

3. Garnish with a slice of dragon fruit.

~ LA BUENA VERBENA ~

Don't be afraid when you see multiple ingredients, they are all useful outside of these recipes. The sweet lemon verbena tea you're about to make is delicious. Make extra.

Glassware: **Coupe**
Garnish: **Lemon Verbena Leaf**

- **1.25 oz Hendrick's gin**
- **.5 oz key lime juice**
- **1 oz lemon verbena tea**
- **.25 oz saffron syrup**

1. Chill a mixing glass with ice or in refrigerator prior to use.

2. Add ingredients to mixing glass and stir until very cold.

3. Pour liquid into a chilled thin coupe glass.

4. Grab a large lemon verbena leaf and make a small slice down the center large enough to allow you to place the leaf on the rim.

Saffron Syrup

- **⅛ tsp crushed Spanish saffron stems**
- **1 cup water**
- **1 cup natural cane sugar**

Bring water, sugar, and saffron to a boil and immediately turn off heat. Let syrup stand until completely cool, then store in refrigerator.

Sweet Lemon Verbena Tea

- **8 oz water**
- **2 oz natural cane sugar**
- **6 large lemon verbena leaves**

Bring water and sugar to boil then add lemon verbena leaves. Let steep 20 minutes then strain and let completely cool. Store refrigerated.

—Tabernilla—

7124 BOB BULLOCK LOOP
LAREDO, TX 78041
(956) 723-7400
TABERNILLALAREDO.COM

Bartenders are my people. I love it when someone with the right kind of talent decides to make cocktails/spirits/bartending their career. That being said, there's something kinda cool about a chef who'll step behind a bar and come up with something. Tabernilla Tapas Bar is a lively tapas restaurant run by Chef Robert Gonzales, a local from Laredo who took off to work in massive programs in New York and Dallas. The cocktail program is, naturally, Spanish heavy with multiple sangrias and a good array of espresso-driven cocktails. It's creative and fun, but not too out there.

— Hye Rum —

I'm a sucker for good wine. I always have been. One of my favorite wineries in Texas was this little hole-in-the-wall place in Deep Ellum (Dallas) called Calais. Ben Calais is a Frenchman turned Texan who can blend the hell out of some wine. Try the Syrah, the Bordeaux, and the Cab Franc to have your mind blown. In fact, this is the Texas wine I usually use in the "Alright pal, I've got some Texas wine, let's do a blind taste test" type challenges that will occasionally appear.

But enough about wine… a few years ago, Ben told me that he was moving to Hye, keeping up his winery, but also going to start making rum. Enter Hye Rum. I got a chance to chat with his co-founder and head distiller, James Davidson, about all things Hye and rum.

So why did you get in to distilling?

About 8 years ago, my Father said he wanted to open a whiskey distillery. I started to study Scotch and other whiskies. I would go to every branding event in the area and joined Scotch groups in order to learn more. While I was widening my pallet, I learned to distill via the internet and books.

How did you and Ben meet?

Ben and I met in 2011 at a pot-luck style dinner party a mutual friend organized. Ben wanted to make rum, but was too busy with his winery to learn to distill and start another business. At the time, I had no experience (or interest) in rum. I just figured it was a random conversation with a guy about the beverage business.

No interest in rum huh? So why the change of heart?

After that conversation, I decided to taste rum. The established "good" rums that a lot of people seemed to like were okay, but seemed overly sweet. After that, I tried some craft rums and they lacked the robust flavor I was used to from drinking Scotch.

Next time I saw Ben, I reported my experience to him. Ben gave me the names of some rums from the French Islands and Jamaica. When I finally secured a couple bottles, I was impressed. They had a lot of flavor and varied greatly from everything else I had tried.

It puzzled me that craft distillers were making near vodka-like rums when the medium had so much to offer. This was a huge motivator for me to move from whiskey to rum. My father often said to me in my youth, "If you don't like it, make it yourself." I felt I could do better then what was readily available.

So why Hye?

It wasn't until 2013 that Ben and I made a hard commitment to pursue a joint venture together. Ben had already purchased land in Hye, Texas for his winery and was in the process of moving there. The wine trail had a lot of traffic and we figured we could catch some of it. Also, Hye was becoming known for some good wineries and Garrison Brother's. We looked in Hye and the surrounding area for 2–3 years before we found our location.

~ PIÑA COLADA ~

Hye Rum
11247 U.S. 290
Hye, TX 78671
(830) 265-5644

hyerum.com

Nothing beats a good piña colada. This is a particularly cool way to serve this classic, and the rum blend is perfect.

Glassware: **Hurricane Glass**
Garnish: **orange slice and a tiny umbrella**

- **3 oz creme of coconut**
- **3 oz pineapple juice**
- **1 oz of Hye White Rum**
- **1.5 oz Hye Dark Rum**
  float on top

1. Blend all ingredients for 30 plus seconds with ice.

2. Serve in a hurricane glass and garnish with an orange slice and a tiny umbrella.

—ANC Alchemy—

Ashley Compton is an East Coast girl turned… Marfaite? Marfinian? She lives in Marfa. Since 2009, Ashley has been making herb-based tinctures, bitters, and various honeys. In 2012, she moved to Marfa and the diversity of her options for ingredients changed dramatically. It opened up a whole new arena of medicinal plants and botanical fauna and has changed the way she's gone about utilizing the natural elements in her work.

All of her products are made in small batches and contain desert-foraged herbs. She also uses chihuahuan desert honey and organic medicinals to flush out the palette of flavors. The bitters are quite unique, which is sometimes hard to do in a bitter, and they provide incredible complexity to cocktails or coffee drinks.

Funny side note, in my past life I was the program director of an indie rock station in Dallas and I got to know Ashley's husband, Andy, when his band Wye Oak played in studio for us. "Civilian" is still one of the greatest songs ever written. But I digress… Ashley was nice enough to provide a recipe for her Brushfire bitters… ANC Alchemy bitters are available online through her website.

— WEST TEXAS —
BRUSHFIRE BITTERS

ANC Alchemy
anc-alchemy.com

Ashley was nice enough to provide a full recipe from gathered ingredients to use in cocktails. This bitters is incredible in an Old Fashioned, particularly when using an agave spirit.

- 2 cups overproof bourbon
- 1 cup dried elderflower
- ½ arbol chile, dried
- ½ ancho chile, dried
- 1/16 cup epazote
- ⅛ cup rosemary, dried
- 20 juniper berries
- ¼ cup bitter orange, dried peel
- ¼ tsp gentian
- ⅛ tsp black walnut leaf
- 2 teaspoons honey

1. In a quart-sized glass jar, combine all of the dried ingredients. Cover with the bourbon and shake well. Let stand in a darkened, cool space for 2 weeks. Shake daily.

2. Strain the infused bourbon into another clean, 1-quart glass jar through cheesecloth. Squeeze any infused alcohol from the cheesecloth into the jar—reserving the solids. Strain again the infused bourbon through new cheesecloth into another clean jar to remove any remaining sediment. Cover the jar and set aside for 1 week.

3. Meanwhile, transfer the solids to a small saucepan. Add 1 cup of water, bring to a boil. Cover and simmer over low heat for 10 minutes; let cool. Pour the combined liquid and solids into a clean, 1-quart glass jar. Cover and let stand in a cool, dark space for 1 week. Shake daily.

4. Double-strain the water mixture through a cheesecloth-lined funnel set over a clean 1-quart glass jar; discard the solid herbs material. Add the infused alcohol and the syrup. Cover and let stand at room temperature for 3 days. Pour the bitters through cheesecloth or strainer. Funnel into 2 or 4 oz dropper bottles. Use to enhance and alchemically-coagulate drinks, or to create a bittered digestif when added to club soda.

~ DESERT SPOON ~

The Blue Door
Recipe: Erica Mann
4610 N Garfield St D
Midland, TX 79705
(432) 218-8793

Sotol means Desert Spoon. Now that we have that covered, I'm so glad there are a few sotol cocktails in this book. Maybe by the end of it, I'll have you convinced that you should give it a try. The Blue Door is at its core a neighborhood bar. In the five years they have been open, they have developed a family that gives back to the community, cheers each other's marriages, babies, and promotions, and supports each other through sickness, hard knocks, and loss. It's kinda like it's a great neighborhood bar in a small(er) Texas town. Owner Erica Mann said, "Being able to experience all of this while also introducing our region to fizzes, egg whites, and crustas, is the cherry in my Manhattan."

Glassware: **Coupe Glass**
Garnish: **Rosemary Sprig**

- 2 oz sotol reposado
- .5 oz Cointreau
- 2 oz ruby red grapefruit juice
- 1 oz lime juice
- .5 oz agave syrup

1. Combine ingredients in a shaker with ice and shake vigorously.

2. Strain into a coupe glass.

3. Garnish with a fresh rosemary sprig.

—A CONVERSATION WITH —
Jason Kosmas

Why would someone who owns one of the hottest bars in New York City move to Dallas?

It was my wife, Carolyn's, mother actually. She had just gone through a divorce and moved back to Texas. Carolyn decided to be with her mom during that time. That was right around the time I realized I was in love with her. She was going back and forth for a couple months and finally says, "Hey, guess what? I moved to Texas."

Long story short, I convinced her to move back to New York, and we opened Employees Only. Then we opened up Macao Trading Company, and then Lola, my first daughter, was born and that was when things really started to change.

So, you moved to Dallas?

I had a plan to do an Employees Only in Austin, back in 2007 or 2008. But It didn't seem like it was a good time for Austin. The culinary movement hadn't really started yet. It wasn't really out there. When I talk to bartenders, they usually have two jobs at least, to make ends meet. Dallas made more sense. We were working on The 86 Co. [Kosmas' spirits company that makes delicious rum, vodka, gin, and tequila] already, and I was writing our cocktail book, *Speakeasy*, pretty ferociously at that time.

How long were you in Dallas and what brought the move to Austin?

My daughter was getting close to a kindergarten. We were like, "Okay, we need to figure out schools…" And all of sudden, Carolyn and I both said, "I think I'm ready to move on." We were still talking about moving to Austin, but in about two years… but then we have

that moment. We're like, "Okay. Once she goes in the school, we're not going to move in a few years." If we want to do this--

Austin is incredible. I really love it. The kids love their school, because it was perfect. I got to know most of the people in bars and restaurants here. Austin is great.

To you, what is a Texas cocktail?

That's a pretty good question. I think Texas cocktails are approachable--they're fun and people go out to drink and have a good time. And what's cool to see is the bartenders here getting to sneak a little creativity and ingenuity into them. In general, I think people in Texas are converting more people into cocktail lovers than either of the coasts.

I mean, look at the restaurants scene. It feels like every restaurant in Texas has a cocktail menu.

And you look at people in Dallas and in Houston, they dine out four nights a week, easily. They're being exposed to it on such a daily basis, more so than people who only go to very pristine cocktail bars. This is the masses. Texas is the democratizing the cocktail.

The whole process of The 86 Company was to grow a cocktail culture and we wanted to help the places who are making cocktails specifically. Then when I moved to Dallas it changed my world and my perspective. I started thinking, "We need to show everybody that cocktails are easy to make." Everyone at the end of the day deserves a good cocktail.

Tradecraft
3737 N Mesa St b
El Paso, TX 79902

"El Paso has a great alcohol history, period. Being right next door to another country, it only takes a few minutes of research to find that the history of our city is ripe with stories of speakeasies, illegal bars, famous patrons, etc. We were the first cocktail forward bar since prohibition. Most bars that you could get a cocktail before us had a small 2-3 drink menu with some fresh fruits and juices, maybe a vodka infusion. Most bars in town have a beer forward mentality and business model. We were the first to take cocktails seriously and base our business on cocktails.

There has been a learning curve for most here, but education is also part of the fun for us. Teaching the history, exploring customer's palates or introducing them to new liquors is incredibly rewarding. We've been open for almost three years now and going strong, so we're definitely doing something right." - Joe Jimenez, the proprietor of Tradecraft.

Glassware: **Nick & Nora**
Garnish: **Orange Peel**

- 1 shot espresso (preferably a Mexican bean)
- 1.5 oz Del Maguey Crema
- .5 oz Del Maguey Vida Mezcal
- .5 oz cinnamon simple syrup

1. Combine ingredients in a shaker with ice and shake vigorously.

2. Strain into a Nick & Nora glass.

3. Garnish with an orange peel.

CRAN-ROSEMARY SYRUP

- 1 cup sugar
- 1 cup water
- 5 rosemary sprigs
- 8 oz 100% cranberry juice

Boil for 5 minutes.

─ PINE BOX ─

Public Haus
Recipe: Kalli Smith, Public Haus
173B Pine St
Abilene, TX 79601
(325) 672-7452

public-haus.com

The first time I ever heard about Public Haus was when I met Drew Garrison at the San Antonio Cocktail Conference. He told me about how he worked for this place in Abilene that was making proper cocktails, and one look at their menu confirmed it. Public Haus was built on the idea that you can introduce a community to cocktails if you make them approachable, make them delicious, and make the community trust you. Drew went on to tell me about how Abilene had been incredibly receptive to a lot of their ideas. And who knows? West Texas cocktails may just wind up being a thing.

Glassware: **Collins Glass**
Garnish: **Rosemary Sprig and Whole Cranberries**

- 1.5 oz gin
- .5 oz Clear Creek Douglas Fir liqueur
- .75 oz lemon juice
- .75 oz Cran-Rosemary syrup

1. Add all ingredients to a collins glass and stir.

2. Garnish with a rosemary sprig and skewered whole cranberries

BEST OF
Texas

LIBER
& Co.

LIBERANDCOMPANY.COM

– Classic –
GUM SYRUP

17 fl oz | Crafted in Austin, TX
503 ml | Makes 40–60 cocktails

ANGOSTURA
aromatic
bitters

44.7% alc./vol.

4 fl. oz. (118 mL)

★ ★

I've always been a fan of those alt-weekly newspaper's "Best of" sections they'll do at the end of every year. "Best ham sandwich on a patio that serves Frosè" or "Best resale shop specializing in toddler sized band shirts." You know the drill. So here's the best of section for the great state of Texas. Just know, the best of the best in Texas is like the best of the best in anything else... it's your preference and taste that matters the most. If you think it's the best, then by golly, it's the best. Here's of some the best that you'll find here.

★ ★

BEST BAR NAMED AFTER AN EPIC BATTLE

To make raspberry-infused tequila, steep 2 pints of raspberries in 1 liter of tequila for a week.

~ MONGOOSE MARGARITA ~

Mongoose Versus Cobra
1011 McGowen St
Houston, TX 77002
(713) 650-6872

mongooseversuscobra.com

This is my favorite bar name, probably ever. And with Better Luck Tomorrow and Ninja Ramen in town as well, the Houston bar name game is certainly strong. The building dates back to 1915, when it was built for the Auditorium Grocery Company, named after the roller skating rink next door. Now, it's a killer craft beer bar with a craft cocktail program that will compete with any in town. The best thing at the bar, however, is not a drink. It's Imperial Andy's Historic Cocktail Tuesday, which they teach bar-goers about "this day in history" by creating four unique cocktails each time. See, mom? I didn't know anything about the rise and fall of Lord Haw Haw (William Joyce) and his trial for betraying the United Kingdom until I started drinking!

Glassware: **Rocks Glass**
Garnish: **Salt, for rimming, Lime Wedge**

- **2 oz raspberry-infused tequila**
- **1 oz lime juice**
- **.5 oz Cointreau**
- **.5 oz agave syrup**

1. Shake and strain the ingredients into a rocks glass rimmed with salt.

2. Garnish with a lime wedge.

— AMY JO JOHNSON —

This is the Amy Jo Johnson and in case you didn't grow up in the mid-1990s, that's the name of the Pink Power Ranger. The drink is a bit spicy and smokey because of the mezcal, a bit sweet and sour because of the shrub, and, appropriately, pink. But it'll kick your butt if you're not careful.

Glassware: **Rocks Glass**
Garnish: **Strawberry and Basil**

- 1.5 oz mezcal
- 1 strawberry
- 3 basil leaves
- .75 oz lime juice
- .75 oz simple syrup
- 1 tsp ume shrub (2 parts umeshu plum wine and 1 part balsamic)

1. Muddle strawberry and basil.

2. Add ingredients and ice to shaker and shake vigorously.

3. Strain into a rocks glass.

4. Garnish with strawberry and basil.

BEST
COCKTAILS AT
A RAMEN
PLACE

—Ninja Ramen—

4219 WASHINGTON AVE
HOUSTON, TX 77007
(281) 888-5873
NINJARAMEN.COM

Ramen and cocktails. A combination that should from hence forth shall never be separated again. Well, if Christopher Huang could have his way, it wouldn't be. Ninja Ramen is super local, incredibly creative. Chris told me that on a trip to Taiwan he went to a series of bars and saw these magical concoctions in coupes everywhere. "I thought, that's it! I'll come back to Houston and I'll open a cocktail bar! We don't have one of those. But by the time I got back and I got invited to this place called Anvil… I decided to regroup and work ramen in to the plan," he told me chuckling.

**BEST
DRAFT COCKTAILS
IN A FOOD
TRUCK PARK**

—Truckyard—

**5624 SEARS ST
DALLAS, TX 75206
(469) 500-0139
TRUCKYARDDALLAS.COM**

When Truckyard hit the Dallas scene, the reaction was overwhelming. Imagine that? Texans loved the idea of craft beer, quick craft cocktails (Truckyard uses a lot of batched cocktails, either utilizing draft systems or often bottling cocktails), and a huge yard full of nothing but park benches and food trucks, all under massive shade trees. It's a patio to end all patios. It's a Texas-style beer garden with decent cocktails. It's one of the easiest places to be. Why didn't we have this since… ever? This isn't rocket science, people, come on. Now, thankfully, Truckyard has reminded everyone just how important a Texas patio is. Inside, they have… 10 seats? I think? Maybe 20, tops. Outside, it's Texas. Beer drinking, Paloma sipping, two-stepping (when there's a band on), Texas.

— FROZEN COCONUT — KEY LIME PIE

We give you the Frozen Coconut Key Lime Pie, the easiest way to impress your friends. And because you should never make just one frozen drink, this is party sized for 8 folks. Or 4 folks. Or just you. I ain't judging. Serves 8.

Glassware: **Pint Glass**
Garnish: **Lime Wedge**

- 1½ cups (12 oz) Keke key lime pie liqueur
- ½ cup (4 oz) Rumhaven coconut water rum
- 6 tbsp (3 oz) lime juice
- 2 tbsp sugar
- 4 cups (32 oz) coconut water

1. Add all ingredients to blender with 2 cups ice.

2. Blend and serve.

— Liber & Co —

Robert and Adam Higginbotham started to see the writing on the wall around 2011. Robert told me, "we noticed that something was missing. While high-end spirits, liqueurs, and bitters meant that everyone could obtain most of what's needed to make better cocktails, there was still a problem for the discerning drinker. An entire ingredient category remained overlooked."

Liber & Co is an absolute requirement for the home bartender. Their gum syrups, grenadine, and orgeat can hang among any housemade versions you'll find. If you need a syrup and Liber & Co. makes it, you're good. These are some of the best cocktail syrups in the country, let alone the state. Liber & Co. is available statewide, as well as a few other states, but are rapidly expanding.

No one offered a way to translate the craft cocktails that people were starting to have out in the wild, so they jumped in. It started as a personal project with all of the founders in three different places, and once they had that first order, they knew they had something. "HEB. That's when I knew it was real. We got our first order from HEB," said Robert, "They're amazing. They try to work specifically with local companies and they support the little guy."

If you see a picture of these guys, you may recognize them from *Billion Dollar Buyer* on CNBC. Producers of the reality show reached out to Liber & Co. with the opportunity to pitch Tillman Fertitta, the owner of Landry's, who operates over 500 properties in 36 states and had just bought this little basketball team in Houston... the Rockets.

"It goes from very low expectations to finding out we were selected... it was crazy. We didn't know anything about TV. We barely knew about the show and now we're wrestling with our landlord to get permission for them to be around for a month," said Robert. "It was weird. It was fun, but it was weird."

— GIN BASIL SMASH —

Liber & Co
2204 Forbes Dr Suite 103
Austin, TX 78754

liberandcompany.com

Fresh basil shines in this simple cocktail and perfectly complements gin's botanicals. This quick and easy cocktail is an example of how using quality ingredients will make you look like you've got the goods!

Glassware: **Rocks Glass**
Garnish: **Fresh Basil**

- **.5 oz Classic Gum Syrup**
- **2 oz gin**
- **2–3 sprigs fresh basil**
- **.75 oz lemon juice**

1. Muddle basil and syrup in a shaker tin.

2. Add lemon juice, gin, and ice and shake for 10 seconds.

3. Fine strain into an ice filled rocks glass.

4. Garnish with a basil leaf.

BEST
WAY TO LOOK LIKE
A MIXOLOGY PRO,
EVEN IF YOU
DON'T KNOW
ANYTHING

BEST BAR
IN AN ALLEY

— THE RUM DIARY —

Atwater Alley
4900 McKinney Ave
Dallas, TX 75205
(469) 893-9400
atwateralley.com

While the "speakeasy" trend is waning, thankfully, one of the best bars in Dallas is still one you'll have to find. In fact, go to their website and all you'll see is a logo and the words "find me." The entrance to Atwater Alley is inside of one. You legitimately have to walk down an alley to an unmarked door. The doorman tends to give the secret away, but it's still pretty cool, nonetheless. Once inside, it's a two-story, cocktail-driven den that absolutely gives you the feeling that only the cool kids know about this one. Their cocktail, The Rum Diary, is slightly bitter but so smooth you'll be making another before you're done with your first.

Glassware: **Coupe Glass**
Garnish: **Lemon Peel**

- 2 oz Brugal 1888
- .5 oz Amaro Nonino
- .5 oz Aperol
- 2 dashes Agnostura bitters

1. Combine all ingredients in a mixing glass.

2. Add ice and stir for 15–30 seconds with a bar spoon.

3. Strain into a coupe and garnish with a lemon peel.

~ THREE EMMAS COCKTAIL ~

Sternewirth at Hotel Emma
136 E Grayson St
San Antonio, TX 78215
(210) 223-7375

thehotelemma.com/culinary/sternewirth

Hotel Emma is, and I say this with no hesitation, the most beautiful hotel I've ever stepped foot into. And hospitality is imperative at their incredible bar, Sternewirth. A dramatic 25-foot vaulted ceiling soars over intimate groupings of sofas, easy chairs, and banquettes arranged to encourage conversation and celebration. Their name-sake cocktail is a tribute to the old Pearl Brewery, in which the hotel now resides. This is the crown jewel of the Pearl district in San Antonio, which may be the crown jewel district in town. Hotel Emma needs to be a bucket list vacation spot. It's truly special.

Glassware: **Nick & Nora**
Garnish: **Basil Leaf**

- 1 oz Pearl Beer and Rose cordial
- 1 oz Amontillado sherry
- .75 oz Botanist gin
- .5 oz lemon juice
- .5 oz grapefruit juice

1. Shake all ingredients together, and strain into glass over fresh cracked ice.

2. Garnish with a basil leaf.

BEST
HOTEL
COCKTAILS

Pearl and Rose Cordial

- 8 12-oz Pearl beers
- 12 cups sugar

1. Slowly pour beer in pot to avoid becoming too foamy. Add the sugar into the pot and turn on low until sugar dissolves. Do not let it get to a full boil.

2. Turn off heat and let cool.

3. Add 36.5 oz rose cordial.

4. Add 2.5 oz rose water.

5. Put into deli containers, label, and date.

BEST
WHISKEY
SELECTION

~ WITHOUT A TRACE ~

Bar 1919
1420 S Alamo St
San Antonio, TX 78204
(210) 227-1420
bar1919.com

Don Marsh was doing classic cocktails in San Antonio before San Antonio had the foggiest clue what classic cocktails that weren't named "margarita" were. Don's influence is felt all over the city, but Bar 1919 ... that's his bar.. It's the bar Don's always wanted, where he can do whatever he wants. The man has over 600 whiskeys, for crying out loud... Bar 1919 is a dark den of possibilities. You have the best selection of whiskeys in Texas, agave only rivaled by certain mezcalarias, and a cocktail menu as good as any in the state. It's a perfect place to explore new spirits and let Don tell you stories about the old days of San Antonio, but don't get him started in on ice density or you may need another drink.

Glassware: **Old Fashioned Glass**
Garnish: Orange Peel

- ♦ **1.5 oz Buffalo Trace bourbon**
- ♦ **.5 oz Amaro Nonino**
- ♦ **.5 oz honey syrup**
- ♦ **.5 oz fresh lemon juice**

1. Add all ingredients into a mixing glass and stir.

2. Lace an old fashioned glass with absinthe and lightly drop a large format cube in the glass.

3. Pourand garnish with an orange peel.

∽ SON OF STAN ∽

This recipe is named after Son of Stan, one of the best acts to come out of Texas in the past few years. In my former life as a porgram director on an indie rock station, Jordan Richardson was one of the mainstays in our rotation. Check out the drink and then check him out on Spotify. It's Divorce Pop at it's finest.

Glassware: **Collins Glass**
Garnish: **Cinnamon, Cinnamon Stick**

- **1.5 oz Lairds Apple Brandy**
- **.75 oz Benedictine**
- **Splash of Dolin Blanc**
- **1 oz apple juice**

1. Combine ingredients in a shaker with ice and shake vigorously.

2. Strain into a collins glass.

3. Top with a splash of soda.

4. Garnish with a dash of cinnamon and a cinnamon stick.

BEST
PLACE TO BUY
VINYL AND COCKTAILS
SIMULTANEOUSLY

—Off the Record—

2716 ELM ST
DALLAS, TX 75226

Some of these new-fangled ideas for cocktail bars are wearing me out; however, the gimmick at Off the Record might be the best one. It's a cocktail bar with a record store in it (not vice versa). You can scan the latest vinyl releases from your favorite local bands, but then you can go grab a drink by the same name. So when I have a chance to throw back a Ronnie Heart or a Zhora (both bands you should check out) then I'm going to jump on it.

BEST
WAY TO ESCAPE
DIRTY SIXTH AND
HAVE A WORLD
CLASS COCKTAIL

DIJON SYRUP (AKA BUCK SAUCE)

- 4 cups honey
- 3 tsps sweet smoked paprika
- 16 tbsp (heaping) Dijon mustard
- 4 oz hot water

Whisk thoroughly to incorporate.

— JOE BUCK —

Midnight Cowboy
Recipe: Bill Norris
313 E 6th St
Austin, TX 78701
(512) 843-2715
midnightcowboymodeling.com

"**M**y favorite thing about the place is the front door. It's the original door from the brothel. It's solid steel and hearing the chaos outside then hearing it shut out by that door is amazing," Bill Norris told me. He's the brain child behind Midnight Cowboy and Alamo Drafthouse's cocktail program. He's also Austin's OG when it comes to cocktails, having overseen the first craft cocktail program in Austin at Fino. The door also has a sliding peep hole that's about 4'9" off the ground because the Madame was a very petite Asian lady. Let me explain. Midnight Cowboy used to be named Midnight Cowboy Modeling and used to be a place where you could get your suspect roughed up, if you know what I mean. It was a house of ill repute run by a petite Asian lady. Now, this reservation-only speakeasy is one of the most incredible cocktail bars in Texas. Pro tip: Ring the name of a famous Savoy bartender for access.

And don't worry… they gutted the place. But they kept the door.

Glassware: **Copper Mule Mug**
Garnish: **Lemon Wheel half-dusted with Cayenne**

- 1.5 oz Balcones Baby Blue
- .5 oz honey Dijon syrup
- .5 oz lemon juice
- Ginger beer

1. Shake all but ginger beer.

2. Pour into mug, top with ginger beer and more ice, swizzle, then garnish.

I f you want a cocktail with some Texas flair, you need to have one made by a Texan. It's as simple as that. Here are some places you can visit for a Texan-made cocktail.

HERBS & RYE

BARTENDER: MATT GRAHAM - AUSTIN
3713 W Sahara Ave
Las Vegas, NV 89102
(702) 982-8036
herbsandrye.com

Matt's been bartending for over 20 years and got his start in the bars on Dirty 6th. "It was also long before craft cocktails were a thing and it helps to remind me not to take things too seriously," he told me. When asked what he would make if someone asked for a Texas cocktail, he said, "I'd throw it out there that I'd whip them up a delicious cocktail using a fresh Bluebonnet-Flower Syrup. Hopefully they'd get the joke since we all grew up believing that it is illegal to pick Bluebonnets off the side of the roads in Texas. I would then make them something along the lines of a whiskey sour or margarita which would hit the spot on a hot summer day."

EVANGELINE

BARTENDER: MICHAEL ANDERSON - LUBBOCK

453 Boulevard of the Allies

Pittsburgh, PA 15219

(412) 339-1870

distrikthotel.com

I met Michael at the St. Charles Exchange in Louisville and within two minutes, we were talking about Texas. That's what you do when you're Texan. He told me that Texas' world-class citrus and approach to food, whether its roasting, charring, or using peppers to bring some heat into the drinks, has impacted the way he builds his menus. He told me, "Texas screams tequila and mezcal at me. If asked, I would steer them in the direction of a margarita or paloma, something with agave."

SAXON + PAROLE

BARTENDER: KIP MOFFITT - HOUSTON

316 Bowery

New York, NY 10012

(212) 254-0350

saxonandparole.com

"My time in Texas has definitely built my career," Kip told me. "It was great working in the Montrose/RiverOaks area since 2005 and seeing all the new bars and restaurants pop up with influences from all over the world." Then we chatted a bit about how Texas has come into its own and created a distinct flavor. He said his version of a Texas cocktail starts with a Paloma, which is perfect. Regarding our home state ingredients, he said, "Texas gets such great citrus and has the best peppers. I didn't appreciate how incredibly flavorful Texas grapefruits were until I was in New York. The spicy peppers aren't spicy up here."

TEARDROP LOUNGE

BARTENDER: NICOLAS FLOWER – DALLAS
1015 NW Everett St
Portland, OR 97209
(503) 445-8109
teardroplounge.com

Nick got his start bartending in NYC but Texas culture has certainly had an impact on the way he approaches the work. "Ultimately, bartending is about hospitality. Where would I be without my parents and grandparents instilling that sense of warmth, friendliness, and generosity? There's never been a Thanksgiving dinner at our house where Mommaw didn't have it under control. I find that comforting and try to replicate it at the bar. Everyone can relax, we've got you," he told me. As for what a Texas cocktail is to him? Frozen margarita.

THE WALK IN

BARTENDER: PHILLIP SMITH – AUSTIN
2727 N Milwaukee Ave,
Chicago, IL 60647
www.thewalkinchicago.com

"To me, the most quintessentially Texas cocktail would be a Paloma. Agave based, Texas grown grapefruit, and perfect on a hot day... What else could you want in a Texas cocktail?" Phillip told me. This Austin native has moved to the Windy City to ply his craft, but the Texan roots still shine through. "Being from Texas has taught me genuine hospitality. It's what I really focus hard on with my new bar team. Genuinely caring about my guests when they walk in the door. It's just of second nature. I think it's in our blood." Go see him in Logan Square.

-INDEX-

-PHOTO CREDITS-

Photos by Nico Martini: pages 48, 51, 52, 56, 59, 60, 62-63, 74, 81, 94, 99, 100, 123, 125, 151, 213, 226, 227, 235, 243, 254, 267, 268, 333, 347, 350-351. Pages 1 and 34: courtesy of Chris Bostick and Claire McCormack Photography; pages 9 and 154: courtesy of Javier Flores; pages 10 and 162: courtesy of Brianna Balducci for Star Chefs; page 17: courtesy of Gina Kirkwood, New Waterloo; pages 22, 30, and 31: courtesy of Mark McDavid; page 32: courtesy of Voyageur Press and Emma Janzen; pages 33 and 69: courtesy of Max Walshe; pages 40, 67, 253, 257, and 259: courtesy of Kody Melton; pages 44-45 and 79: courtesy of SungJoon Koo; page 72: courtesy of Alex Gregg, Moving Sidewalk; page 77: courtesy of Mark Koelsch; pages 82-83, 86, 107, 352, and 356-357: courtesy of Julie Soefer Photography; pages 90 and 93: courtesy of Whitmeyer's Distilling Co., Houston, TX; page 97: courtesy of Rich Bailey; page 104: courtesy of Kristen Gyorfi; page 111: courtesy of Houston Farris, Head Distiller; page 117: courtesy of Steven Salazar; page 127: courtesy of Jessica Sanders, drink. well.; pages 128 and 131: courtesy of Tito's Handmade Vodka; Page 139: Still Austin Whiskey Co. Page 140: Amanda Sprague, Cultivate Public Relations. page 143: courtesy of Revolution Spirits by Miguel Lecuona; page 144: courtesy of Amanda Turner; page 148: courtesy of Mike Groener; page 152: courtesy of Justin Lavenue and Dennis Gobis; page 158: courtesy of Small Victory; page 160: courtesy of SoCo Ginger Beer; page 165: courtesy of Nate Powell; page 167: courtesy of Mark Weatherford; pages 168-169 and 200: courtesy of Tony Alvarez; page 172: courtesy of Jones Long; page 175: courtesy of Jared Norton; page 176: courtesy of Chad Yar-

brough; page 179: courtesy of Western Son Distillery; page 180: courtesy of Lauren Gebhardt, Bottled in Bond Cocktail Parlour and Kitchen; page 183: courtesy of Tawn Carranza; page 186: courtesy of Cowtown Paparazzi; pages 188 and 190: courtesy of Gabe Sanchez, owner, Black Swan Saloon; page 193: courtesy of Chris Dempsey, D&D Shrubs and Syrups Co.; page 195: courtesy of Clark Cabus Photography; page 197: courtesy of Herman Marshall; page 205: courtesy of Edgar Campbell; pages 206 and 209: courtesy of Firestone & Robertson Distilling Co.; page 210: courtesy of Eric Pulido, Paschall Bar; page 214: courtesy of Amber Davidson, Bird Café; page 219: courtesy of Omar YeeFoon; pages 222 and 358: courtesy of Courtney Bradford; page 231: courtesy of Brad Hensarling, The Usual; pages 232, 236, and 263: courtesy of Front Burner Restaurants; pages 238-239, 264, and 266: courtesy of Hilmy Creative; pages 244 and 292: courtesy of Jason Risner Photography; page 270: courtesy of Azar Distilling; page 273: courtesy of Jonathan Rogers; page 278: courtesy of Black Pearl; page 281: courtesy of Alina Mikos & Mary Ellen "Mellen" Julsen; pages 283 and 285: courtesy of Deux South Creative; page 289: courtesy of Metropolitan; page 291: courtesy of Dripping Springs; pages 295 and 297: courtesy of Laura Merrian; page 299: courtesy of Christi Brinkman; page 302: courtesy of Justin Bowers, Captiv Creative; page 305: courtesy of Dan Garrison; page 308: courtesy of Daniel Copado; page 311: courtesy of Roberto Gonzalez, Tabernilla—Bar de Tapas, Laredo, TX; pages 312 and 313: courtesy of Stephanie Houston; page 317: courtesy of Ash Compton; page 318: courtesy of Erica Mann; page 323: courtesy of Bobby Gallagher/Lens Hungry/TradeCraft; page 324: courtesy of Alexandra Chabek (@7angerine); pages 326-327, 336, 337, and 339: courtesy of Juliet Beletic, EJB Creative; page 330: courtesy of Mongoose Vs Cobra; page 334: courtesy of Truck Yard; page 340: courtesy of Austin Marc Graff; page 343: courtesy of Beth Smith; page 348: courtesy of Tracy Rowland.

All other images used under official license from Shutterstock.com.

—ABOUT THE AUTHOR—

Nico Martini lives in Dallas with his wife, Sarah, and toddler, Beckett. He is a former guest lecturer at The University of Texas at Dallas; founded Hypeworthy, a marketing agency; co-founded Bar Draught; and presented seminars for Bar Institute, San Antonio Cocktail Conference, and Portland Cocktail Week. Nico has been on tour with hippie jugglers, has performed in wild west comedy gunfight shows, and is a member of the Lincoln Center Director's Lab. He received, but didn't accept, a hockey scholarship to Penn State and recently gave a TEDx talk on cocktails. All of these statements are true, and yes, Martini is his legal last name.

–ABOUT CIDER MILL PRESS BOOK PUBLISHERS–

Good ideas ripen with time. From seed to harvest, Cider Mill Press brings fine reading, information, and entertainment together between the covers of its creatively crafted books. Our Cider Mill bears fruit twice a year, publishing a new crop of titles each spring and fall.

"Where Good Books Are Ready for Press"

Visit us on the Web at
www.cidermillpress.com

or write to us at
PO Box 454
12 Spring St.
Kennebunkport, Maine 04046

YELLOW ━━━━━
East Texas & Gulf Ry.
Groveton, Lufkin & Northern Ry.
Missouri Pacific Lines:
  Asherton & Gulf Ry.
  Beaumont, Sour Lake & Western Ry.
  Houston & Brazos Valley Ry.
  International-Great Northern R.R.
  Orange & Northwestern R.R.
  Rio Grande City Ry.
  San Antonio, Uvalde & Gulf R.R.
  St. Louis, Brownsville & Mexico Ry.
  Sugar Land Ry.
  Moscow, Camden & San Augustine Ry.
  Texas & Pacific R.R.
  Denison & Pacific Suburban Ry.
  Texas Southeastern R.R.
  Weatherford, Mineral Wells & North-
    western Ry.

ORANGE ━━━━━
  Angelina & Neches River R.R.
  Denison, Bonham & New Orleans R.R.
  Fort Worth & Denver City Ry.
  Texas City Terminal Ry.
  Texas Midland R.R.
  Trinity & Brazos Valley Ry.
  Wichita Falls, Ranger & Fort Worth R.R.
  Wichita Valley Ry.

BROWN ━━━━━
  Chicago, Rock Island & Gulf Ry.
  Eastland, Wichita Falls & Gulf R.R.
  Nacogdoches & Southeastern R.R.
  Paris & Mt. Pleasant R.R.